A Divine Calling

About the Author

A graduate of Trinity College with Masters degrees in business and ecumenical theology, Soline has appeared many times on radio and television, including on *The Late Late Show* and *Upfront with Katie Hannon*, was featured in *New Yorker* magazine and has written for *The Irish Times* and numerous other publications. She lives in Dublin.

A Divine Calling

One Woman's Life-Long Battle for Equality in the Catholic Church

Soline Humbert

The Liffey Press

Published by
The Liffey Press
'Clareville', 307 Clontarf Road
Dublin D03 PO46, Ireland
www.theliffeypress.com

© 2025 Soline Humbert

A catalogue record of this book is
available from the British Library.

ISBN 978-1-0686645-6-4

All rights reserved. No part of this publication may be reproduced or transmitted in any form or by any means, including photocopying and recording, without written permission of the publisher. Such written permission must also be obtained before any part of this publication is stored in a retrieval system of any nature. Requests for permission should be directed to The Liffey Press, 'Clareville', 307 Clontarf Road, Dublin D03 PO46 Ireland.

Printed in Bulgaria by Pulsio Print

Contents

Foreword by Mary McAleese	vii
Prologue	2
1. A French Childhood	7
2. Ireland's Call and God's Call	35
3. The Lord's Year of Favour	64
4. Brothers And Sisters In Christ	75
5. A Woman of Sorrow	103
6. A Woman at the Altar	132
7. Women's Ordination Worldwide	161
8. Mary of Magdala	181
9. No Woman, No Church	207
10. Epilogue	236
Select Bibliography	239
Acknowledgements	240

And the Holy One answered me:
Write down the vision
And make it plain on tablets
That those who read it may run with it.
For the vision is yet for the appointed time.
It will not fail
But will be fulfilled in due time.
If it delays, wait for it.
For it will come and will not be deferred.

Habbakuk 2:2-3

Foreword

Mary McAleese

John XXIII's encyclical *Pacem in Terris* first pointed to the advancement of women as one of the most important 'signs of the times'.

> ... they are demanding both in domestic and in public life the rights and duties which belong to them as human persons[1]. . . . The longstanding inferiority complex of certain classes because of their economic and social status, sex, or position in the State, and the corresponding superiority complex of other classes, is rapidly becoming a thing of the past.[2]

At the Second Vatican Council, Archbishop Paul Hallinan of Atlanta warned the bishops to stop perpetuating 'the secondary place accorded to women in the Church of the 20th century' and to avoid the Church being a 'late-comer in [their] social, political and economic development'.[3]

---

[1] John XXIII encyclical *Pacem in Terris*, 11 April 1963, n. 41.

[2] Ibid. n. 43.

[3] Cf. Fr. P. Jordan OSB, NCWC News Rome correspondent, 'Changes proposed in role of women in the Church', posted 12 October 1965. Cf. https://vaticaniiat50.wordpress.com /2015/10/12/changes-proposed-in-role-of-women-in-the-church/

The Council's decree *Apostolicam Actuositatem* said it was important that women 'participate more widely ... in the various sectors of the Church's apostolate'.[4] The Council's pastoral constitution *Gaudium et Spes* said the elimination of discrimination based on gender was a priority.[5] Paul VI even commissioned a study on women in Church and Society.[6]

It seemed possible then that the post-Conciliar Church was on the way to acknowledging full equality for its 600 million female members. For generations women faced outrageous struggles for gender equality and for their civil and human rights in the civic sphere in many countries, and still do. The Church's magisterium had never distinguished itself as a champion of women's civil rights, whether the right to vote, to become lawyers, doctors, take part in sports, own their own property, control their own fertility, limit the size of their families, or work outside the home. But now it faced a real 'kairos' moment. Would the magisterium internalise in its teachings the inalienable right to gender equality set out in the Universal Declaration of Human Rights 1948? Would it affirm the inalienable human rights of all church members to freedom of conscience, expression, opinion, belief and religion, including the right to change religion?

The answer we now know, loud and clear, is that post the debacle of the papal encyclical *Humanae Vitae* (1969), when

---

[4] Second Vatican Council, *Apostolicam Actuositatem* decree, 18 November 1965, n. 9 in AAS 58 (1966), 846-.

[5] Cf. Second Vatican Council, Pastoral Constitution *Gaudium et Spes*, 7 December 1965, n. 29 in AAS 58 (1966), 1048-1049

[6] It reported in 1976.

millions of Catholics and especially women rejected its ban on artificial contraception, the magisterium burrowed even deeper into its traditional misogyny and autocracy, doubling down in a series of documents from 1976 onwards,[7] on the ban on ordination of women to the diaconate and priesthood, threatening excommunication for those who challenged it and insinuating quite wrongly that the ban was based on infallible teaching.

There were other post-Conciliar signs of irredentist magisterial sexism. Paul VI had redesignated the roles of stable lector, stable acolyte and permanent deacon as now suitable for the laity, just not female laity. Laity, both male and female, could be temporary altar servers but individual bishops and parish priests could ban female altar servers in their dioceses or parishes. The ludicrous nature of those bans was highlighted at the Voices of Faith Conference in March 2018 and the magisterium was challenged to explain their continuance, and to explain how it planned to include women in decision making in the Church when they were excluded from the very priesthood through which all decisions were made.

Under growing pressure for reform from the People of God, and facing a crisis of credibility evident in the dwindling Church numbers and vocations in the West, Pope Francis made a number of barely minimal changes in hopes of calming the building storm. He removed the bans on women as stable lectors and acolytes and set up two commissions to report on women and the diaconate,

---

[7] Congregation for the Doctrine of the Faith, declaration Inter Insigniores On the Question of the Ordination of Women to the Ministerial Priesthood, 15 October 1976.

neither of which have been published. He even appeared to encourage freedom of speech and an open agenda at his Synod on Synodality, but three years in and a million words later any hopes of revisiting the exclusion of women from ordination, as demanded by the faithful all over the globe, were dashed by the Pope himself, in his uniquely untrustworthy flip-flop, populist, revert-to-autocratic style.

In July 2023, Pope Francis acknowledged that the theological foundation on which the ban on ordination of women sits, lacks 'a clear and authoritative doctrine' which 'has not yet been fully developed'. However he then insisted that while: 'It is not a dogmatic definition . . . it must be adhered to by all. No one can publicly contradict it and yet it can be a subject of study.'[8] The sheer brutal nature of this diktat provoked considerable public contradiction. Church members who have the inalienable right to their own opinions and to freedom of expression let Pope Francis know that the days of the magisterium telling the faithful what they 'must' adhere to and must not say publicly are long, long gone.

Ten months later, in April 2024, as the public contradiction grew in volume, the response came from Pope Francis not in any recognisable Church or synodal process but in an interview with American CBS television. There he emphatically ruled out the ordination of women to diaconate and priesthood. There was no reference to any

---

[8] Pope Francis, Response to five dubbia, 11 July 2023, published by Dicastery for the Doctrine of the Faith, available at: https://www.vatican.va/roman_curia/congregations/cfaith/documents/rc_con_cfaith_risposta-dubia-2023_en.html.

study (though there have been many which conclude the ban on women's ordination has no legitimate biblical or theological basis). Having read the works which justify the ban, I was compelled to politely describe them as 'codology dressed up as theology'.

The latest attempt to close down debate came from Cardinal Hollerich, Synod relator: 'When discussing hot-button issues such as women in the church it is important not to be a lobby group. Lobbying is not part of church culture; it should not be. We have other tools, like prayer, discussion, listening to each other.'[9] Bless! Check the history books dear Cardinal and there you will find the suffragettes fighting misogyny, the civil rights activists fighting sectarianism, homophobia and racism, those who marched for religious freedom including Catholic Emancipation, were lobby groups by any other name and indeed people of prayer, discussion and listening who were ignored and repressed by people of prayer, discussion and listening to themselves, and in the end it is their truth which is marching on leaving the hierarchy of the Catholic Church barely visible in the rear view mirror, out of touch and running out of time.

One of those lobby groups was founded by Soline Humbert, not just to argue for the ordination of women but to draw attention to the untold and tragic story of the many women called to priesthood by God who were and are denied admission by toxic man-made laws from a magisterium whose claims to divine legitimacy and infallibility are a classic case of the emperor who had no clothes. Soline

---

[9] Cardinal Hollerich, interview in *Crux*, 2 August 1983.

is one of those women and here she lays bare the profound suffering she has endured wanting to serve God as God wants and the Church needs, but being rebuffed, ignored, labelled, stereotyped, as if God only talks to clerics and like them has no time for women as equals. Who could believe in such a God?

A new generation, educated in human rights, experienced in the history of gender equality, capable of critiquing poorly structured magisterial teaching, will likely wonder why Soline still bothers. Here she tells us in language that is at once simple and yet clearly the distillation of years of prayer and deliberation. She believes in God, in Christ, in the great commandment to love one another, in its transformative power in a world rendered dysfunctional by the hatreds that are the core of sexism, racism, sectarianism and homophobia.

The Catholic Church has been and is still guilty of transmitting those hatreds even while doing huge good in the world as the biggest NGO and a key influencer across five continents and many cultures. For all her life Soline has patiently witnessed to the power of God's effusive, endless love and to the wonder of a life called by God to be a witness, a powerful sign of contradiction. She is, to paraphrase Seamus Heaney's magnificent prophetic voice in his poem 'From the Canton of Expectation', the 'one among us who never swerved from all her instincts told her was right action, who stood her ground in the indicative, whose boat will lift when the cloudburst happens'.[10]

---

[10] Seamus Heaney, 'From the Canton of Expectation', in *New Selected Poems*, Faber and Faber, 237.

Foreword

The Synod on Synodality dodged the cloudburst when the issue of women's ordination was removed from its agenda and parked in the Dicastery for the Doctrine of the Faith. But the cloudburst is coming and Soline's solid boat will lift while the holed barque of the misogynistic magisterium will sink in ignominy and irrelevance.

For my mother,
      whose love and faith
           guided my first steps
                  and lit up the path ahead.

A short time at my side,
      forever in my heart.

'How long does it take to become a priest?' asked the child.

'A lifetime,' replied the old priest.

But if you are a little girl, it will take several lifetimes, generations. When I first heard the call to priesthood fifty years ago, I wondered how I would be able to live with it in a Church which denied it.

'You were born forty years too early!' was a comment I often heard then.

Well, I was born and I had to live that calling, *now*!

Half a century and six popes later, in the middle of a global and national synodal process, the door to women's ordination is still stubbornly closed, a vestige of our centuries-old subordination. And yet, I didn't just survive, I flourished against the odds in this hostile Church environment.

In this memoir I share my response to that calling which has taken me to many surprising places. It is the story of a spiritual and vocational journey into the unknown, on a path filled with pain and wonder, joy and grief, strength and vulnerability, tears and laughter. It is about my inner life and my public advocacy. Above all, it is a story of faith in the One with whom nothing is impossible, and it is filled with unquenchable hope.

Prologue

It was a grey January morning in 1994 in Dublin and I was about to leave the house when the phone rang. It was my husband Colm from his office: 'Your interview is in today's *Irish Times*, nearly a whole page, large photo.'

'Today! Of all the days to publish.'

'The nuncio must have choked on his cornflakes when he opened his newspaper with his breakfast,' Colm joked.

'I'll know soon enough.'

'Good luck.'

With that I headed for the nunciature. I had requested a meeting only the previous week and the nuncio, Archbishop Emanuele Gerada, had replied positively with an alacrity I was unaccustomed to on the part of high ranking churchmen. He was obviously as eager to meet me as I was to meet him, although probably for a different reason.

It was the first and only time I was inside a nunciature. While I was waiting in the office, I looked around. There were no religious objects or pictures in sight. I could only see a framed photo of Pope John Paul II. It was a reminder that this was an embassy, representing a state, the Holy See, of which the pope was the head.

I remembered also what a friend, a religious sister, had told me upon hearing I was meeting the nuncio: 'He has

Romero's blood on his hands,' referring to his previous role as Nuncio in El Salvador when Archbishop Romero had been murdered.

After a few minutes the nuncio, a small Maltese man, made his entrance, unsmiling, obviously in a bad mood. Perhaps because I unconsciously feared that *The Irish Times* article was like a red rag to a bull, that's how he appeared to me. Was I about to be gored?

He came straight to the point: 'What do you want?'

'I want to meet the pope.'

'The pope doesn't meet people . . . like you. He meets bishops, cardinals, important people.'

That was me put back in my place. I felt like a five-year-old.

'And why do you want to meet the pope?'

'I want to tell him that there are women who have a sense of vocation to the priesthood. I am one of them.'

'And you think the pope should change his plan for the Church because of you?'

'No, not because of me, but because of God. It's God's Church.'

After a short silence: 'Have you tried the religious life, you could be a nun, a sister . . .'

He said it in a tone which made me think of somebody throwing a bone to a dog to stop it barking.

'It's not the same vocation. I believe God is calling me to the priesthood.'

At that stage I did wonder whether he had read the interview after all, since it showed clearly I was married with children. I could hardly leave them all for a convent, or perhaps he thought anything would do to get rid of me.

But the nuncio was not interested in me whatsoever, which he made very clear. He never asked me one personal question. I was a nobody.

'I have written to the pope several times but I haven't got a reply.'

'Your letters do not deserve a reply,' he stated categorically, 'but, in the very unlikely event the pope would respond to you, the reply would come first to me, and I would transmit it to you.'

And that was the end of that.

What I hadn't told the nuncio was that, unbeknownst to him, one of my letters to the pope had gone through the nunciature's diplomatic bag. Although addressed 'Private and Confidential' it had obviously been intercepted by the Secretary of State, Cardinal Sodano, who replied with a nondescript card with the assurance of prayers.

Coffee was then served. I noticed my hand was trembling so much it was very difficult to bring the small espresso cup to my lips without sloshing the coffee. I had to use both hands to drink.

To fill in the awkward silence I was inspired to comment on his first name, Emanuele, which was also the middle name of one of our sons. That's when he opened up, much to my surprise. 'I am the second son, my mother gave me that name.' It was obvious that it wasn't a good thing to him. Second in parental affection too?

He then went on to complain at length about the nunciature having been moved out of the Phoenix Park onto the Navan Road, in the middle of nowhere, so far away from Ballsbridge where all the embassies were. I listened silently to him pouring out his grievances, thinking, 'if that is the only thing he has to complain about . . .'

When he had exhausted the subject, remembering I was French, he then proudly told me he had been to Lisieux and that he had even had the privilege of celebrating Mass in St Thérèse's cell in Carmel.

I seized the occasion to ask him in a cheerful voice: 'And did you know she wanted to be a priest?' He groaned and glared at me.

At that stage he signalled our meeting was over. He walked with me to the front door and he waited there while I got into my car. I enjoyed giving him a big wave as I drove out past him.

I had the words of the 'Lourdes Magnificat' on my lips:

> The world will call me blest
> And ponder my story
> For in me is made manifest
> God's greatness and his glory

On my way home I bought a copy of *The Irish Times*. There I was, with our two young sons, happily smiling and laughing under a very big headline:

Fighting Sexism in the Church

and the subtitle:

A Report on the formation of an Irish group whose aim is the ordination of women in the Catholic Church.

The article concluded with my words: 'Ideally, I would like to bring joy to a currently stultified Church.'

The nuncio had shown me both his hierarchical power and its complete emptiness. There was absolutely no joy in him, a very unhappy man. Later, in February, I was moved to send him a card, with a quote from St Thérèse of Lisieux. I felt he was in urgent need of her spiritual help!

There is a slogan in use among supporters of women's ordination: 'Ordain women or stop baptising them!' It contains much wisdom because, of course, the roots of my request to the nuncio and my actions as reported in *The Irish Times* went all the way to my baptism. The trouble, if trouble it was, originated in that sacrament. Its subversive power shouldn't be underestimated. It had revealed itself very gradually in my life until it had led me to this day when I confronted the pope's representative with a truth so compelling I couldn't ignore or deny it.

1.

A French Childhood

I was baptised a Christian – another Christ – in the Catholic Church on 26 August 1956, three weeks after my birth in Valenciennes, in the north of France. It was a joyous occasion for my parents who, after having a son three years previously, were now welcoming a little girl.

I was named after Saint Soline, who had been martyred in Chartres in the early centuries of Christianity. As a Christening present I was given a ceramic plaque representing the dark haired young woman with a crown of laurels in one hand and a sword in the other. She became a permanent presence on the wall of my bedroom as I pondered her life of which only the bare outlines were known: the laurels and the sword represented her martyrdom, as she had been beheaded for refusing to marry a pagan prince. In the first version of her story I heard it was her father who had executed her. It was a stark warning of what happened to young women who challenged the patriarchal order, and also a reminder of the cost demanded by fidelity to God and to oneself. I was in awe of her courage but admired it from a safe distance. The truth is that she intimidated me.

The name Soline comes from the Latin *Solemnis*, meaning solemn. It was my mother who had chosen it, a very unusual name at the time, perhaps because she had encountered it on the annual student pilgrimage to Chartres or because of a writer named Claire Sainte-Soline. There was a book by her on my parents' bookshelves, *Le dimanche des rameaux* (*Palm Sunday*) with her name prominent on the spine. For many decades this was the only instance of my name I encountered anywhere, and I still have not met another Soline in the flesh!

I would have been named after Yseult (Isolde in English) if my father, a romantic who had read the legend of Tristan and Isolde, had had his way. However, while I wasn't named after that Irish princess, I eventually did become an Irish citizen.

For middle names I was given both my grandmothers', which happened to be those of the two greatest women in the Gospels, Mary and Madeleine.

ಬ ಬ ಬ

MY MOTHER, MICHELINE HUMBERT, an only child, was from Lorraine in the east of France. She met my father, René Vatinel from Normandy, when they were both studying in Paris after the war. She was training as a Montessori teacher and he was studying engineering. They were married on Monday, 16 August 1951, in the Basilica of Notre Dame de Sion. It was the day after the feast of the Assumption of Mary, which had always been a great celebration in France (and still is a public holiday). But this 15 August had been exceptionally festive as the first feast day since the Assumption of Mary into Heaven had been proclaimed a dogma of the Church by Pope Pius XII on 1 November 1950.

A French Childhood

Notre Dame de Sion is a sanctuary dedicated to Mary on top of the Hill of Sion. It is an impressive sight as the hill rises high above the plain of Lorraine. The Hill of Sion was celebrated in 1913 in a famous novel by Maurice Barres, *La Colline Inspirée* (*The Inspired Hill*), as 'one of the places where the Spirit blows'. The veneration of Mary in Sion goes back to the fourth century, replacing veneration to male and female divinities.

As a young child, whenever I was on holidays at my maternal grandmother's we would go to the Hill of Sion. It would be my first pilgrimage, although of course it wasn't called as such. It was a day out, an expedition, as we took the bus and then climbed up the hill to the Basilica.

'That's where your parents got married,' she would tell me. Their wedding photo of them coming out of the church was in our home, so I could easily visualise their younger selves, my mother with her long white veil beside my father. We would say a prayer, light a candle, and then have refreshments outside while we rested, admiring the wonderful panorama all around us.

I knew that my life was somehow linked to this place, that my birth was the fruit of their wedded lives and love. So when at Mass the hymn 'Rejoice Daughter of Sion' was sung, I believed it was addressed to me in a special way. I was a daughter of Sion: my parents' wedding in Sion made me so!

Early beliefs are hard to dislodge, and sometimes contain a grain of truth 'hidden from the learned and the wise'. Even after being in the Holy Land, it is still the Sion of my childhood which comes first to my mind and, in my heart, I am forever that daughter of Sion called to rejoice!

A Divine Calling

ೞ   ೞ   ೞ

MY EARLIEST CLEAR MEMORY of church was of attending a service one evening in the middle of February 1961. I was four and a half years old. The large old church dedicated to Saint Symphorien in Versailles, where we now lived, was full. We sat and prayed for a while, then the congregation stood up and moved in a queue to the altar. When our turn came, I was delighted to see my parents motioning me to go up with them. Usually I was left behind, alone on the bench, as they went up with my older brother to receive Communion.

Now, at long last, my time had come too, and I knew exactly what to do. As I reached the steps of the sanctuary where the priest stood, I carefully closed my eyes and pulled out my tongue. To my shock and horror I felt the priest's thumb grinding something on my forehead while he muttered something about dust. But on my tongue, nothing. I closed my mouth and turned around to go back to my seat.

As I opened my eyes I was amazed to see everybody with big black smudges of dirt on their foreheads. So that's what I had on my face too! I was absolutely disgusted. I felt badly let down.

I was obviously too young to receive the bread of life, but old enough to be reminded of my mortality. Even at that early age and with no theology, it didn't go down well with me. First impressions matter.

ೞ   ೞ   ೞ

MY EARLIEST MEMORY OF MARY goes back to when I was five. I am at school, it's winter. I am sitting at my desk with a piece of dark coloured paper, a pot of white glue, and blue and pink wool, already cut in small strands. I am concentrating on my task. It's Advent and we are preparing for Christmas.

Little by little as I glue the blue wool, one strand at a time, on the outline traced by the teacher, her dress appears. And then, carefully, the pink wool for her face. Voilà! I am making Mary, the mother of baby Jesus. A child's Mary. What has remained is a feeling of wonder and a deep, close communion with Her, as she emerges from under my small sticky fingertips. She is motherly, tenderly Love.

ɞ   ɞ   ɞ

AT LAST, THE TIME CAME FOR ME to make my first Holy Communion at the age of six, on 27 April 1963 in the church Notre Dame of Versailles. The imposing, ornate church, built in 1686 on the orders of Louis XIV, the Sun King, had been the parish church for the palace and the royal family. It was so large it could have been a cathedral. It wasn't our own parish church, but was nearer to the Catholic school where I was a pupil.

I remember some of the preparation for our Communion, including very practical aspects. Communion was still received on the tongue, and we practiced, with unconsecrated hosts, on how to hold our tongues out and swallow the host. It couldn't be chewed, and if it stuck to the inside of one's mouth (as it always did), how to use one's tongue (not fingers!) to dislodge it. A very un-natural way to be fed!

I must have made my first confession beforehand, but have absolutely no recollection of it. Was it in the Church or in a small room in the school where I do remember making my confessions later? Was it to the chaplain, a tall, erudite

Jesuit, Bernard de Boissière, a gentle and kind man? Much later I discovered that he had been a close friend and disciple of Maurice Zundel, the Swiss theologian and mystic who wrote of God's tenderness. That didn't surprise me.

On the day we sang the hymn we had learnt, 'I have received the living God and my heart is filled with joy'. It expressed perfectly what I felt as I went up and received: I was filled with joy!

I can see that joy on my face in the photos as I smile under my simple flower crown, in my little red blazer over my pleated white skirt and embroidered blouse, the handiwork of my grandmother.

One of the religious presents I received (there was no tradition of Communion or Confirmation money) was a small framed crucifix, which has followed me everywhere. I still have it on my bedroom wall.

Our teacher gave us a holy picture representing the Last Supper by Fra Angelico and wrote on mine, 'For Soline to receive Communion often'. She signed it, as well as some of my fellow communicants. Every year I mark the anniversary of that spring day when I first received 'My Lord and my God' in the words we had been taught to say. A seed of that great Mystery of Love that is the Eucharist had been planted in me. In time it would flourish in a most surprising way.

ಉ ಉ ಉ

BOTH MY PARENTS WERE COMMITTED Catholics, my mother especially so. She had been a Montessori teacher and now, when we came to live in Le Chesnay, near Versailles, she worked as a parish catechist. This was, of course, unpaid in a voluntary capacity, as most women's work in the church was at the time, and still is. But it was something she believed in and enjoyed doing. This meant that the parish priest often came to our house to discuss things with her. He was received like any other adult visitor, there was no fawning or special treatment, but there is one amusing anecdote which remains with me.

One afternoon my grandmother had come to visit and felt the need to voice her disapproval of my posture: 'Do not sit with your knees turned in!'

To my great surprise, my mother spoke up for me: 'Leave her alone. Monsieur le Curé was here this morning, and that's the way he was sitting.'

My grandmother, displeased, said nothing but I was chuffed. I was sitting the same way as the parish priest! I still smile at the thought.

୪୨ ୪୨ ୪୨

I WAS SEVEN WHEN MY MOTHER became ill. Actually, to my child's eyes, at first she didn't appear very ill at all. But I could sense it was grave the way my parents and the other adults reacted: 'It's breast cancer.'

I hardly knew what breasts were, I didn't have any yet, and as for cancer I just knew it was a bad illness and there were charitable collections for it ('the fight against cancer'). It must have been a frightening time for my parents. I knew too little to understand, but our lives were turned upside down. My parents, faced with the illness and the demands of the treatment, organised to send me to a children's home for two weeks.

A Divine Calling

It was in Taverny, another Parisian suburb. It was bewilderingly traumatic for me. It wasn't the first time I was away from home, but before it had been with my grandparents. Now I was on my own, in an institution, with complete strangers. Some of the children were there long term because they had special needs. I had never slept in a large dormitory, or been in communal toilets and bathrooms or eaten in a refectory. I had been parachuted into a strange world.

One incident has stayed in my mind. I wrote to my parents telling them I had a cold, which was true. I innocently handed over my letter for posting but didn't know that our letters were being read. The following morning I was informed, 'Since you have told your parents you have a cold, you will be confined to bed all day.' I felt utterly betrayed. How dare they read my private correspondence? They had no right, as I saw it. And then punish me for telling the truth. I had a cold, not a bad one, but I did have one.

I think it is there that I discovered adult hypocrisy. The head of the children's home had been very different when greeting me in the presence of my parents.

It was a very long two weeks. I was so relieved when my parents came to collect me. But the childhood trauma remained. For many years I couldn't bear to hear the name 'Taverny'.

The reality was that it was a deeply traumatic time for all the family. My grandmother, my mother's mother, uprooted herself from her native east of France where she had lived all her life to move closer to us to give support. She bought a small apartment on the other side of Versailles, and I moved in with her for the school year 1964-65. I now had a long walk and a suburban train journey four times a day, but at least I could stay in my school.

I slept in my grandmother's bedroom. It cannot have been easy for her to have a lively eight-year-old around, but she looked after me well.

She had a large oil painting of a Madonna and child, a copy by the Italian painter Bellini, and I used to look at it while she said her prayers before switching off the light at night. She recited the 'Memorare', 'Remember O most gracious Virgin Mary', every night and I wondered: Why does the Virgin Mary need to be reminded all the time? Has she got such a bad memory she needs to be prompted, 'Remember!' over and over again?

Whatever the Virgin Mary's memory, mine never extended to remembering the words of the 'Memorare', beyond the first sentence. I guessed She would know the rest without my prompting.

My mother spent Christmas in hospital. Friends gave her a small plastic crib she could put on her bedside locker. It is no work of art and has had to be glued back together, but I inherited it and put it on my own bedside table every Christmas.

The months passed by, my mother came through a long and painful treatment, and I went back home. In the summer I caught a glimpse of her new swimsuit, with the left breast filled with foam padding: That was the only sign I ever saw of the surgical operation she had undergone. Life resumed as 'normal', but of course my mother was now 'in remission' and the shadow of cancer hung over us.

My school progress hadn't suffered. Much later I saw that my religion teacher had described me in her report as 'deep', which at first surprised me for there was quite a lot of the tomboy in me, according to the expression in use then. But on reflection, she was quite insightful, because while I played football and climbed trees and roller skated, I also spent hours reading and pondering things. Some of the questions which occupied me were: 'What if I had been born in a different country or at a different time in history? Who would I be? What would my life be like?'

I was not pious or devout, but I did like reading about the lives of saints. We had several at home, written for children, with pictures. We had the martyrs of Uganda (recently canonised in 1964), Joseph Sarto (Pope Pius X), Vincent de Paul, the children at Fatima, St Bernadette Soubirous, and of course St Joan of Arc had pride of place, including in our history books.

I was particularly fond of her, and not just because she came from Lorraine like my mother. She was much more my kind of girl. In our dressing up games I dressed more readily as a knight than a princess. Not for me to wait passively at home for prince charming to come; I wanted adventure and action.

There was a church nearby dedicated to St Joan, where we sometimes went for Mass. On the wall high above the altar there were large colourful frescoes of scenes of her life, from her calling while minding sheep to her burning at the stake, and then her welcome into heaven by St Michael, St Catherine and St Marguerite. It was a very impressive scene which engraved itself in my mind as I gazed upon it while the priest preached long sermons. There, in front of my eyes, was a young woman, in armour, called by God to do something only men did. How subversive was that?

A French Childhood

While I liked reading the stories of the saints, there seemed to be a gulf between them and me. I knew I didn't have any of their fervour, and certainly not their 'good behaviour'. The one Bible story from the Old Testament which made a lasting impression on me was from my school reading book: The calling of the boy Samuel in the Temple in the middle of the night.

It fascinated me, and filled me with wonder how God could call a child like me. But of course nothing like that ever happened to me or anybody I knew. 'In those days the word of the Lord was rare, there were not many visions' (Samuel 3:1). It seemed to me this was the case now in France in the 1960s. Still, I wondered what it was like to hear God in the middle of the night, but it was beyond me to even imagine it.

I liked a lot of the Gospel stories, like Jesus healing people, but the one which resonated most was the Annunciation to Mary. An older friend had offered me a choice of 'holy pictures' on her Profession of Faith day, and I had picked the one with Fra Angelico's 'Annunciation'. In 1982, when visiting the Prado in Madrid, I had the joy of contemplating the original and bought a copy to frame. No other painting has ever spoken to me as deeply over my lifetime.

୫ଡ ୫ଡ ୫ଡ

I WAS CONFIRMED ON 31 MAY 1967, the last day of the month dedicated to Mary. With the post-Vatican II revision of the liturgical calendar in use in 1969 it became the date for the celebration of the Feast of the Visitation, when Mary, just pregnant with Jesus, visits her older cousin Elisabeth, six months pregnant with John the Baptist. When the two women meet, Elisabeth is filled with the Holy Spirit, and Mary proclaims her Magnificat. It is a feast which I love and celebrate it every year together with the anniversary of my confirmation.

I was only ten when I was confirmed. In the only photo I have of the day I stand, alone, in the little dark blue velvet dress my grandmother had made for me. My hair is short, and I have a solemn look on my face. What is happening inside me? The Confirmation took place in the same church where I had made my first Holy Communion, Notre Dame, in Versailles. The bishop at the time had a name which delighted us children: Monseigneur Renard (Fox).

My sponsor wanted to give me a book on my matron saint (a traditional present) but couldn't find one on Saint Soline, too obscure, and instead presented me with one on Saint Veronica. So, while in France we do not take a Confirmation name, I adopted this one. I loved the story of Veronica and her gesture of tender compassion for Jesus, wiping his bloodied face with her veil, and the meaning of her name: true icon, image, from the imprint of Jesus' face on her veil.

We had been well prepared for our confirmation, and had done a retreat. I took it very seriously and looked forward to receiving this precious gift of the Holy Spirit, which meant that I expected something of the first Pentecost events as described in the Bible to take place. Not tongues of fire and a mighty wind, but I did expect some tangible inner transformation as had happened to the early disciples. So I was somewhat disappointed the following days when I realised I wasn't one bit holier! I would have to let go of my childish magic wand theology and learn about the very slow release miracle.

But the parish gave us each a gift of a paperback copy of the Four Gospels, and I started immersing myself in it; I even read it once in the bath! I still have it, with its undulating pages from water damage and my childish pencil markings. I was now fully launched on a lifelong love of scripture. It would sustain me in the years ahead, because what I didn't know on that sunny May day was that this was my last religious celebration with my mother present. Come Holy Spirit!

༄ ༄ ༄

THE FOLLOWING YEAR, 1968, France was in turmoil with student protests and social unrest which started in May. The president, Charles de Gaulle, dissolved the National Assembly. In June, the time had come for me to make my *Profession de Foi* (Profession of Faith), which entails the renewal of my baptismal promises.

It is normally a happy family celebration, but for us it was overshadowed by my mother's deteriorating condition as the cancer had come back, this time in her liver. She was in hospital and wouldn't be able to be with us.

The ceremony was in two parts, a short evening one and then the longer one on Saturday, again in Notre Dame of Versailles, the same church where I had made my First Holy Communion and Confirmation. We all wore white albs and a pectoral cross. The girls also wore a simple white veil. While I was happy wearing the alb, I did not like the veil and took it off as soon as I could. It's still on my head in the official photo, but I am happily bare-headed in my father's photos at home afterwards.

After the shorter Friday evening ceremony we went straight to visit my mother in hospital so that she could see me in my lovely white alb. On getting out of the car I brushed past a pole covered in tar and got a big black stain on my sleeve!

I processed into the church in the morning, proudly holding a tall lit candle. The priest in charge of the ceremony, l'abbé Leclerc, had kindly offered to record it so that my mother could listen to it afterwards. Not being able to be present was painful for her.

After the church ceremony our small family group went for a nice lunch in the open air in the beautiful palace gardens. It was a luminous, sunny June day but we all felt acutely my mother's absence and the unspoken question hung in the air: Would she ever be able to join us again?

The parish gave us a copy of the whole New Testament, with Christ the Pantocrator on the cover. I still have it, now well worn. I also received a leather bound missal from my parents. It was in both Latin and French, published at this transition time in the liturgy. It is not so well worn, as it became quickly redundant. But the deer at the foot of the cross on its cover always spoke to me: Like a deer thirsting for running streams, my soul longs for you.

ೞ   ೞ   ೞ

THE LAST TIME I SAW MY MOTHER at home was at the end of July 1968. Earlier in the month my father had taken my brother and myself for a two week holiday at the seaside in Vendée at La Croix de Vie. My mother was in remission and had gained back enough weight to be able to come by train to join us for the second week there. We didn't know it but it would be our last holiday together. We then went home and at the beginning of August I left with my Godfather, his wife and baby daughter for a month holiday in the Vosges. I celebrated my twelfth birthday with them on 4 August.

My parents had gone to Switzerland for a holiday. The international news was disturbing. On the radio I heard of the Soviet tanks invading Czechoslovakia, crushing the Prague spring. Then came more disturbing news closer to home: My mother had relapsed while on holidays and my father had had to bring her to the hospital nearby in France.

My mother's health deteriorated. She was brought by ambulance to a clinic in a small town, Ecquevilly, west of Paris, where she got whatever meagre palliative care was available then.

My father, my brother and I were now all back at home. My father went back to work and I started preparing myself for going back to school. I busied myself buying clothes and my new schoolbooks, covering them with colourful protective shiny paper.

At the weekends we would collect my grandmother and drive to Ecquevilly, which appeared to be miles away in the middle of nowhere, certainly nowhere familiar. My memories are of a very short time in my mother's room and a long time sitting with my brother on a bench in the garden while my father and grandmother were inside. My mother by then was very thin and yellow-looking. Her arms were bruised and punctured by syringe marks. Even though she was only 43, she looked like a much older woman. A lot of her hair was grey and she was a shadow of herself. It was hard to believe that six weeks earlier she was at the beach with us.

Sitting on that bench, not far from under her window, I played in the gravel. I can still hear the crunching sound. My brother and I didn't speak much. We were at the periphery of this adult world of illness and hospital care. Waiting, bored, anxious, more waiting. Was she going to get better soon? When will she be able to go home? We wondered, each with our own silent thoughts.

My grandparents, my father's parents, and my aunt visited my mother before returning to Tunisia where they were living. Several decades later my aunt still cried recounting it. She said that there was so little pain-relieving care for my mother and she had no phone in her bedroom. My aunt said to her, 'Why don't you ask for one, you could speak with your husband and children.'

But she replied, 'If I ask for a phone, it will have to be taken from somebody else.' And she didn't want that.

Summer was coming to an end; we were nearing the Autumn equinox. On the last day of the holidays I woke up with a fever. I fretted: Will I be well enough tomorrow, or will I miss the first day back at school? I had been looking forward to it, but for today I would have to stay in bed. My brother stayed too to mind me while my father and grandmother went to Ecquevilly.

After they had left the fever abated and I started feeling better. I heard my father coming home and I looked up from my bed when he entered my bedroom.

'Maman is not suffering any more,' he told me. I was relieved. She is better. He must have seen the hopeful look on my face showing I misunderstood for he added: 'Maman is dead'. Three words which ended my childhood.

My mother had become very unwell, her heart failed and she died alone in her room, shortly before my father and grandmother arrived. It must have been a terrible shock for them. None of us had said our good-byes to her.

The next few days are a blur. Grief can bring on its own form of insane thoughts to protect us from a painful reality. Jesus resurrected Lazarus; perhaps he could do it for my mother? Why do I remember my father getting me to pray for this? Did he actually believe it? Who knows what happened in the despair and chaos of our world turned upside down?

My mysterious fever left me as quickly as it had arrived. Somehow I was bodily connected to my mother's agony and death. My grandmother sewed a black crepe armband on my grey coat for the funeral. I wore it until I grew out of the coat.

In the church I saw my school mates who had started the new school year without me. And in front of the altar there was a closed coffin. My mother was in it but I never saw her dead. It was my first funeral, the first time I saw a coffin.

After the Mass we went to the graveyard. Rows of tombs and a big hole in the earth. We were numb with grief. I cry, my father cries, but my brother who is now fifteen doesn't. We were all burying parts of ourselves. We must have eaten somewhere after the burial, but I cannot remember.

Life resumed. I went back to school. The Protestant neighbours from below brought us desserts. There was no counselling and I knew nothing about grief and all its effects. We each endured it as we could.

For a long time I would see a middle-aged woman in the distance and think it was my mother, forgetting she was dead. My heart would lift and then I would be crushed again. I didn't know it was a common reaction which would fade in time. I had entered the strange land of loss without a map, and on the cusp of puberty, itself a new territory. There were hard years ahead.

The day of my mother's death, 22 September 1968, there was a complete solar eclipse recorded. But the person I loved the most and who loved me was gone. My world had suddenly turned darker and colder.

ಬ ಬ ಬ

MY MOTHER'S DEATH COINCIDED with my entering adolescence, and all its inner transformations. I would have to navigate these uncharted waters without her.

My faith would have undergone some change anyway, for I was a reflective child, but my mother's death brought about urgent questioning: As I stood at my mother's grave, where was God?

My initial response had been similar to that of Martha upon the death of her brother Lazarus, saying to Jesus, 'If you had been there my mother wouldn't have died!' I had to hold on to the hard, cold fact that my mother had died but remember Jesus' promise: 'The one who believes in me will never die' (John 11: 26).

How could I reconcile these two conflicting realities in my twelve-year-old mind and heart? I held on to both, although they were in fierce tension. Somehow my mother's death didn't lead me to stop believing, but it eventually transformed my faith.

It was around that time that I adopted a personal motto, 'I have overcome the world', just as Jesus said to his followers, 'In the world you will have troubles, but take heart, I have overcome the world' (John 16:33).

As I looked at the last photo of my mother, standing in the ground of the hospital four weeks before her death, I couldn't but wonder how serene and even luminous she looked. Thin and older than her forty-three years, but smiling. Beside her my father's face is filled with pain and anxiety.

Several years later my paternal grandparents gave me a letter my mother had sent them a few months before her death. In it she wrote that it had been hard, but she had found the grace to let go of her life and was at peace.

When I read it I understood why she looked as she did in that photo. She wasn't just smiling at the camera but, invisibly, at the One beyond. She was already straddling another realm. She had done her grieving and let go. We now had to do the same, and it would take each of us on very different paths. Mine would take me to Ireland. There I would find 'my place of Resurrection' as the early Celtic saints used to say.

One of the best things I did after my mother's death was to join the Girl Guides (Guides de France), which was a Catholic organisation but with a post-Vatican II spirituality, open to the world. Our leader was a young woman who had been injured in a fire while rescuing people. Her courage, both at the time of the rescue and afterwards facing the world while badly disfigured, was an inspiration to us. She involved us in the traditional scouting activities of camping and hiking, which I loved, but also in social justice and charitable work. I visited a black family in one of the poorer areas of the town, and it opened my eyes to the harsh realities of racism and social inequality. I was reading books on racism in South Africa and in the US (*Cry the Beloved Country* by Alan Paton and *Black Boy* by Richard Wright) but this was right on my door step and in the air I breathed.

Later, in my last years at school, I volunteered to help immigrant workers fill out forms. They were all men, mostly from North Africa and Portugal, often with little literacy or French. As we sat in an empty school classroom, I wondered how it was for them to have a young girl helping them with all this paperwork, what it did for their self-esteem. They seemed content enough, but still?

I didn't particularly like the paperwork, the red tape, but I liked them, the people, and I was glad I could be of some small help. I knew they left their countries and families because of unemployment, that they lived in our town in crowded hostels and that they were doing the jobs considered too menial by the French and yet still essential. I saw them on the building sites and collecting our bins, sweeping our streets.

I knew they were looked down upon and called derogatory names. They always left grateful with a smile, so it was fulfilling work, but deep down I was ashamed at the pervasive inequality and racism.

We also went to Germany one summer and walked from Koblenz to Mainz, where I had my first ecumenical encounter. One Sunday we found out there was no Catholic Church nearby, only a Lutheran Church . Our leader didn't hesitate and brought us to it. It was a long church service, all in German! But it was my introduction to ecumenism and planted a seed.

A French Childhood

When the time came to make my Scout promise in 1970 I had an issue about the traditional formula. I discussed it with the priest who was our chaplain: I could promise to serve God, to serve the Church , but I couldn't promise to serve my fatherland. Why? Because I wasn't sure I would be staying in France. I had spent three weeks in Ireland and was thinking of moving there. I took my promise very seriously; it was a solemn public commitment. The chaplain understood my reasoning so we agreed I could promise 'to serve the human community in which I live'. This, I reckoned, could extend beyond borders to the whole world.

I also had the choice of a Gospel reading for the Mass. I didn't hesitate: I chose the Sermon on the Mount, the Beatitudes. It was already my favourite Gospel.

When I turned fifteen I served for two years as a Cub Scout leader, looking after boys between the ages of 8 and 11. I enjoyed helping children discover new skills, the wonders of life in the wild, group activities and games. It was a wholesome environment and I am grateful to the scouting movement. Something of it remains in me to this day.

Whenever I wasn't scouting, I read voraciously. Most of my pocket money was spent buying books of all kinds. The author who inspired me most was a Catholic layman, Gilbert Cesbron. His spirituality reflected that of the Second Vatican Council. My parents had some of his earlier books, novels on worker priests, and I bought his later ones. He had one on the Beatitudes.

I enjoyed the books at home by Jacques Maritain and Henri de Lubac. The title of one of the latter's books fascinated me: *Le Drame de l'humaniste Athée* (*The Drama of Atheist Humanism*). I also read Teilhard de Chardin and Georges Bernanos, who wrote *The Diary of a Country Priest*.

At school where I majored in French and Philosophy for my baccalauréat, we studied the writings of Plato, Rousseau, Camus, Mauriac, Sartre, Freud, Marx, Husserl, Blondel, Jankélevitch etc. A lot of men!

We had residential spiritual retreats with the Sisters of the Cenacle, which I appreciated. Their convent in Versailles in the middle of a large park was an oasis of tranquillity for reflection, prayer and sharing. They had a very up to date approach to spirituality and adolescents.

I was also a member of the Jeunesse Étudiante Chrétienne (JEC) and we met monthly in a small group with a priest for prayer and discussion on all kind of topics. We had what we called 'Partage D'Evangile' where we reflected on and shared Gospel passages. I was too young to appreciate this post-Vatican II period for the exciting time it was, as I knew little else, but I certainly did benefit from it.

I went with a parish group for a weekend to the Cistercian abbey in Boquen in Britanny. It had become a laboratory for a radical experiment in monastic life and liturgy under the leadership of the controversial young prior, Bernard Besret, who had been an expert theologian (*peritus*) at Vatican II. I was one of the youngest, in my early teens, so largely unaware of what was at stake, but it also left a mark.

We slept, boys and girls, in our sleeping bags on the ground in one of the rooms of that very old abbey. We attended one of the discussions with Bernard Besret and I listened very attentively to him, trying to understand and follow. So much was very new to me. It was there I first heard of Zen. I was visibly concentrating so hard that

Bernard Besret pointed me out as the young lady who is like 'The Thinker' by Rodin. It was said very kindly and lightheartedly, but of course I blushed. I wasn't aware I had adopted the pose of a famous sculpture! But thinking was something I did a lot of in those years, trying to figure out the world, God, myself, everything!

Bernard Besret was deposed as prior by Rome in late 1969, but stayed on until 1974 when a more traditional female community of Cistercians was brought in to replace the men.

Another year I made my first visit to Taizé in Burgundy where the Council of Youth was in full swing. It was Easter but still bitterly cold. Pope Paul VI had described the Taizé ecumenical community as that 'little spring', but weather-wise it was wintry with snow on the ground and frozen waterpipes. We slept with our coats on in the tents.

But there was indeed a wonderful springtime energy. One of the boys in my tent with whom I shared my thoughts was a luminous Lutheran German whose name, Pascal, was in tune with the Paschal Mystery we were celebrating. Afterwards he became a pastor and we corresponded for several years.

As young people, girls and boys soon to enter adult lives, our voices were valued. We could share our lives, our hopes, and discover how others from different countries or denominations lived. There was also the liturgical beauty and simplicity, the singing and the times of silent prayer. To have tasted Taizé in the early 1970s was a great, lasting, blessing. For years I was on the mailing list for the *Taizé Letter* with its news and spiritual reflections. I would go back in the mid-1970s, in the heat of a Burgundy summer this time, and again it would nourish my soul deeply. But we were told repeatedly, and we knew, that we had to experience our Christian lives wherever we were, in the ordinary messiness and complexity of the every day. That was the challenge.

The main subject in my last year at school was philosophy. There was a rumour that our teacher, a young woman, was a Freudian and a Marxist. She may have been as both Marx and Freud were on the curriculum as was their critique of religion. Thus one day she asked the class the following question: 'How does God define self in the Old Testament?'

As nobody answered she challenged us, half mockingly, 'You are Catholic girls, in a Catholic school, and you don't know your Bible?'

I was stung. Most of my fellow pupils couldn't have cared less, but I did care. In the ensuing silence, I dug deep into myself and finally emerged with an answer: 'I am who I am,' I called out.

The teacher looked at me. 'Yes, indeed, that's it. I am who I am.'

ಣ ಣ ಣ

THE EVENT WHICH WOULD MOST change my life happened nine months after my mother's death. The summer was approaching and my father was wondering what to do with me during the long school holidays. That's when the young woman who had prepared me for my Profession of Faith, and who was also an English teacher, suggested I should come with her to Ireland for three weeks in July. She was bringing a group of children who would be staying with families as paying guests.

It was a great adventure, my first plane journey, my first trip abroad without my family. I was twelve, nearly thirteen, I didn't know this holiday would alter the course of my life. Our little group arrived in Tullow, County Carlow, a very small town. I called it a village!

My host family, the Deegans, were an older couple with a ten-year-old daughter, and they ran a grocery store on Main Street. I was made very welcome and immediately fell in love with the people and the country. By the end of the three weeks I was hooked!

The first Sunday I was leaving to go to Mass when my hosts called me back and told me I needed to wear something on my head. I couldn't understand why since I hadn't worn anything on my head in church for years. Surely, if that was good enough for God in France . . . . But they insisted and gave me an orange crochet beret, which I thought was hideous and removed the minute I was around the corner.

When I entered the Church of the Holy Rosary, I caused an immediate sensation. As I was taking in the strange arrangement of the women and girls on one side, the men and boys on the other, I heard whispering voices and heads turning to stare at me: 'Mammy, she has nothing on her head.'

Every female over the age of two had a scarf, a hat, a beret, something on their head. I suddenly felt very self-conscious, though not enough to put on the orange beret! At least I complied and sat with the females, a concession to the local gender segregation.

When the time came for Communion, I went up and put out my hands, but the priest indicated only on the tongue. I had already forgotten how strange that was.

The family wondered whether I was really Catholic. I didn't know about the Angelus (we didn't have the bells on the radio in France), and we definitely didn't all kneel down in the kitchen in the evening to say the Rosary. In fact, I am not sure I had ever said the Rosary at that stage. While they thought I was barely Catholic, I thought Irish Catholicism was old-fashioned, heavy on rules and pious devotions and fairly joyless. But I didn't have much to do with it.

Every weekday morning we had English classes in the local convent of the Brigidine Sisters beside the church. It was in Tullow that the order founded by St Brigid of Kildare had been re-established by Bishop Daniel Delaney. At the time, an acorn had been brought back from Kildare and planted in the ground of the convent where there was now a majestic oak tree.

I liked my holidays in Tullow so much that I came back the following year. After that, my host family having moved, I spent two more summers in Gorey, County Wexford, with Anne and Fintan Duggan.

During the school year I pined for my holidays in Ireland. In a corner of a copy book I penned a (bad) verse about my longing, which I still know by heart:

> Mais j'aime trop l'Irlande, ce doux pays,
> pour ne pas songer à y passer le reste de ma vie.
> C'est sur cette terre, par le malheur tant de fois labourée,
> Qu'un jour renaîtra la grande liberté .

> But I love Ireland too much, that sweet country,
> Not to dream of spending there the rest of my life.
> It is on that land so often harrowed by misfortune
> That one day the great freedom will be reborn.

I would have to make the dream come true. In 1973, my last year at school, I applied to all colleges in Ireland. I was accepted first by Trinity College Dublin. Now the Irish adventure would start in earnest.

ಬ ಬ ಬ

BUT BEFORE I MOVE ON TO OTHER shores, I must relate two incidents from my adolescent years which left a mark on me. The first was within the family and I look upon it as my first run in with patriarchy.

I was spending a fortnight's holidays with my paternal grandparents at the seaside. They now lived in North Africa (Algeria and then Tunisia) together with my aunt and young cousin, but came back to France every summer. It was the first time I had seen them since before my mother's death. I was enjoying the holidays until one day at lunch the conversation between the adults touched on the subject of the Arab population. My grandfather made a sweeping statement saying that 'the Arabs are thieves'. I should have ignored it and kept eating my chips, but at thirteen I had ideas of my own and I felt his statement was unjust: 'You cannot say *all* are thieves, that's racist.'

There was absolute consternation. How did I dare contradict my grandfather who got apoplectic and, feeling unwell, left the table to go and lie down. My grandmother chided me: 'See, you have made Grandpa sick, it's your fault he isn't well.' My aunt chimed in, 'You are awful, you're giving a terrible example to your little cousin.'

I went to my room, feeling miserable and lonely, unable to cope with the guilt and shame piled on to me. I had challenged the patriarch of the family. It would take me many years before I could shed the ingrained sense I was 'bad' for challenging statements by patriarchs, especially those who speak for God.

The second incident was when I was sixteen. I needed to have an eye test so I went to the ophthalmologist. He examined my eyes, and afterwards asked me what I was doing after school. I said I was off to Ireland. At that he pulled from a drawer all kinds of photos and carefully put them in front of me. I looked. They were photos of foetuses! I froze.

I think he said something about abortion, but I didn't take it in. I was horrified, not by the pictures, which I hardly looked at, but by him and his action. What gave him the right to do that to me, to take advantage of me?

I was speechless and couldn't leave fast enough. I felt dirty, abused. On the way home I reflected he must have confused Ireland with England, or perhaps he showed these to all girls and women? After the initial shock I felt very angry. How dare he? Why didn't I speak up and tell him what he was doing was abusive?

I knew what he had done was unprofessional, but I was a sixteen-year-old girl and he was a respected practitioner. What could I do? I didn't say anything to my father, but I swore to myself I would never go back to that ophthalmologist. The main benefit was that I would soon become immune to these abusive methods.

2.

Ireland's Call and God's Call

When I turned seventeen the time came to uproot myself. The soil had been loosened by my mother's death and my four holidays in Ireland. I was ready to say goodbye to my father, brother, grandmother, best friend, country and my childhood home.

I arrived at Dublin airport in September 1973 with one small blue steel trunk. I was directed to register as an alien with immigration services in Dublin Castle before enrolling in Trinity College as a student of History and Political Science. I had visited it once, as a twelve-year-old tourist, to see the famous Book of Kells. Now I belonged here; the adventure I had long dreamt about had started. I was filled with a heady mixture of excitement and trepidation.

I was staying in lodgings ('digs') in a house in Rathgar, sharing a room with an Irish student and an American one. I had only been in Dublin before on a few short day trips and had to find my way in a new bustling city. While I was exactly where I wanted to be, it was far from easy. It was no holiday! My youthful self had not measured the challenges facing me: the lack of home comforts, the acute loneliness, especially on Sundays, the homesickness when communications were so sparse: Landline telephone calls were expensive and only for emergencies, and letters took a week to reach their destination.

I had been a pupil in the same small school from the age of five to my baccalauréat so it was a big jump to a large university in a different culture and language. It was after Christmas before my English was up to speed to be able to take notes at lectures. I knew very little about Irish and English history. I struggled and there were many times, as winter approached and the grey days got even wetter and shorter, when I questioned my decision to put myself through such hardship. My exile was voluntary and I could have ended it at any time and returned home, but something kept me here. As I persevered, I slowly found my feet and my tongue in that strange new land.

When the new year came I was more settled, had made friends and gone hiking in Connemara with the college climbing club. I was now able to enjoy some of the fun and freedom of student life, with one important exception in this pub-dominated culture: I still didn't drink!

ಬ ಬ ಬ

In March I was back home in France during spring break. An American friend came to visit and I decided to show him Chartres Cathedral. The ancient cathedral, dedicated to Mary, is a jewel of gothic architecture famed for its stained glass, and more recently for its labyrinth. It is a moving and impressive sight as it rises from the fertile plain around it, a tall ship on a sea of wheat. I had visited there several times as a child. It had a special place in my heart, and not just because of the special connection with Saint Soline.

While visiting the cathedral and admiring its beauty, I took some time to kneel in prayer before the statue of the Black Madonna and lit a candle. Nothing special happened, but a short time afterwards, back in Dublin, I had an experience which I always linked to that silent prayer.

I call it now an awakening, but I wouldn't have described it as such then because I had no word for it. It was new and completely unexpected. I was ambushed by an incredible, powerful, overwhelming sensation of being flooded by love. I had been in love before, I had had boyfriends, but that was both similar and utterly different.

The love that was filling me was both deeply personal and also universal. I was loved because the whole world was loved. Of course I knew of God's love, having been raised a Christian, but it had been in the realm of second hand knowledge: now I knew it in the depths of my being.

It was indescribable then, and it still is. A year later I read a book, *Il Fait Dieu* (*It's God-ing*), by a gifted young French writer, Didier Decoin, describing a similar experience and at the same time confessing that his most brilliant words were but a pale reflection of the splendour of that all encompassing love.

I knew absolutely nothing of mystical experiences though in fact I had had a foretaste when I was about fourteen. One day, in my bedroom, listening to a piece of classical music on my record player I was ravished. It pierced my soul with its exquisite beauty. So much so that I wrote on a small piece of paper just four words, 'Divine Music, Divine Musicians'. I folded the paper and kept it in my bedside locker for a long time as a reminder. That divine music had opened up something in me, a resonance with the great beyond. But now, in 1974, this was more than a glimpse: It lasted several light-filled blissful weeks, when I was floating on air.

The landing was to be both abrupt and painful.

ಲಿ   ಲಿ   ಲಿ

FOLLOWING ON FROM THIS INFLOW of God's love I felt the need to respond by going to confession, to receive the sacrament of Reconciliation. I used to regularly pass by Harrington Street church on the bus on my way to Trinity College and decided that's where I would go. I went in one Saturday and entered the dark confessional box, filled with God's love and joy. When I emerged I was profoundly distraught and in floods of tears. I had to take some time to compose myself enough to be able to go back outside and face the world.

What had happened? I couldn't make sense of it. I had told the priest I hadn't been to confession for a few years, probably a bad start in his book. After beginning the confession of my sins he must have picked up on my French accent as he unleashed a long, angry tirade. I don't remember his exact words, but the gist of it was that I had sexually corrupted the Irish boys. To him, I was obviously just a French whore . . .

What he based this on, besides my accent and my gender, I have no idea; it was completely irrational. The irony was that I was still sexually inexperienced at the time.

The priest eventually gave me absolution but his gruff dismissal with the formulaic 'Go in Peace' meant nothing. It couldn't undo the damage of his words and the turmoil it left me in. I had felt peace coming in; he completely robbed me of it.

Later I asked myself: Why didn't I object? Why didn't I speak up, interrupt him, stand up and leave? Why did I allow him to treat me like that? But the reality was that I was only seventeen, a girl, and he was a priest who was at least forty years older than me. And I was on my knees, in the middle of receiving a sacrament, frozen and in complete shock. I had never experienced anything like that abuse in all my confessions in France.

I couldn't articulate it at the time, but I felt deeply violated, a form of verbal rape. He had dumped all his own sexual issues on me, made me into a scapegoat, and then released me burdened with his sins. When I left, I felt unclean.

It was my first confession in Ireland, and the last time I would enter the darkness of a confession box to open my soul to a stranger. Afterwards, I would only do so with priests I knew well, like the college chaplains.

The trauma of that confession stayed with me a long time. I could never re-enter that church, and just the sight of it was a painful reminder. Twenty years later, while attending my dentist across the road, I went into the church and in the quiet darkness prayed for that priest, whether still living or now dead, who knew so little of God's love, tenderness and mercy. I also thanked God that this painful experience hadn't destroyed my faith. It had, however, contributed to my understanding of the many disturbing realities in Church life.

ಬ ಬ ಬ

While my choice of the Harrington Street Church to open my tender soul had been a mistake, I was more fortunate with the college chaplains I got to know. Trinity College, founded by Queen Elizabeth in 1592, had originally been a Church of Ireland University and it was only in 1970 that the Catholic bishops lifted the ban on Catholics studying there. At the same time, Archbishop John Charles McQuaid appointed Father Brendan Heffernan as chaplain. In 1973, another chaplain, Father Eamonn McCarthy, joined him.

The two young priests had embraced the Second Vatican Council reforms wholeheartedly. They were open-minded, open-hearted men, dedicated pastors committed to creating a vibrant community. We called them by their first names, dropping the 'father' title. They were generous with their time, often going beyond the call of duty. There was an open door policy in the chaplaincy rooms which were often filled with students, not all Catholics or even Christians. It offered much more than free tea and bad instant coffee: there was companionship, serious discussions, plenty of fun and banter, and a place to rest when life was too hectic or difficult. I made friendships there which have lasted to this day. It was a safe space and it became for me a home from home. Two of these lifelong friends, Siobhán Fleming and Dónal Denham, invited me to their wedding in December 1974. It was my first Irish wedding and I was deeply moved to be included.

The most precious gift Brendan and Eamonn gave me was that of a listening ear, and not just when I was in college. Back in France for holidays I would write to them and they always replied, thoughtfully addressing my concerns. They were a much needed lifeline for the 'crazy, mixed-up kid' I was, in my own words.

The joyful spiritual experience in the spring was now just a memory, one which had opened up an abyss in my soul. The high tide of God's love which had lifted me so powerfully had receded, leaving me high and dry. But with it came a most surprising gift, though it certainly didn't seem like a gift at the time!

Sometime in late 1974 I became aware of a calling to the priesthood (or presbyteral ministry, to use the proper description) surfacing in me. It was the last thing I expected and nothing, absolutely nothing, had prepared me for it.

I had grown up in the Catholic Church where it was believed that only men were called by God to be priests. I had never heard it being discussed, I had never questioned it, still less challenged it. I just accepted that some men had a vocation to be priests or monks and that some women had a vocation to be nuns. It was as simple as that, and it didn't bother me. I had never felt any interest in the religious life whatsoever. It just wasn't on my radar.

There were no priests or nuns in my family, except distant cousins. In the aftermath of Vatican II, priests were no longer put on a pedestal. I also had plenty of positive experiences with lay people living their faith deeply in a variety of ways. All my catechists had been laypeople. Did I even know of the existence of women pastors in other denominations? I certainly had never met one.

I didn't know what I would work at when I finished college, but the honours degree was four years long so I had plenty of time to figure it out. I had followed my heart in studying history in Ireland and my immediate focus was to study hard, pass the exams and get a good degree to launch me on a fulfilling career path. I had a fair bit of idealism and commitment to social justice and human rights, but how I would live them out was unknown.

That's where I was when I suddenly 'heard' this call. Even as I write these lines half a century later, there is something which remains mysterious as I try to understand it. It's a bit like trying to pin down mercury: it resists every effort to explain it, including explaining it away!

How did I 'hear' the call? I don't know, but I *did* hear it. Some people can pinpoint an event, an exact time, a word of scripture, but I can't. It just seems to have slowly emerged, like a rock under water becoming visible at low tide. And yes, the call was as solid and immovable as rock. It was no fleeting airy thing I could ignore or brush away. It was full of paradox:

It came from within me, but from beyond me, not of me.

It was a desire I didn't choose or want.

It was something I couldn't understand or even imagine.

I had never heard of a woman being a priest. There was no role model with whom I could identify or who could validate what I was experiencing. Being male was the essence of the priesthood. That's all I knew. Indeed, it was the centuries-old belief of the Christian community to which I belonged and was shared by everyone, at least as far as I knew. So how could I possibly 'hear' that calling? It didn't make sense.

The level of disturbance it provoked in me was seismic. If God called only men to priesthood and I was 'hearing' this call, then what was I? Was I male after all? But I knew I was a girl. I had no gender issue (not that transgender issues were discussed in 1974 Ireland), but I couldn't get my head around it. Was I crazy? What did it all mean?

So my gender was certain but the calling was getting stronger. What was I to do? How could I reconcile the two? Well, I prayed and cried, and prayed and cried some more. My strongest memory is of praying before the Blessed Sacrament over and over again: 'Do not call me. Your Church doesn't want me.'

Tectonic plates had shifted. I had somehow come to believe, to accept, that it was indeed God calling me, a girl, but I was the only one in the world to believe it so where did that leave me? Profoundly alone, dislocated, with a massive identity crisis. Who was I? How could I live?

The one scripture passage from that time which remains vividly with me, one that I grappled with, is the Gospel passage (John 21:18) where Jesus tells Peter:

> When you were young you put on your own belt and you went where you wanted. When you are old, somebody else will put a belt around you and lead you where you would rather not go.

Whenever I read that quote I am immediately back in my small room in Trinity Hall (my cell!) where I spent a whole night in anguish struggling with it: I was Peter.

The whole thing precipitated a kind of a nervous breakdown. I went to see the college psychiatrist, who was kind and did what he could. He asked questions and listened over several sessions, but after a while he said to me: 'Do you talk with the chaplains?' I said I did, so he just said, 'Continue talking with them.'

I did talk with the chaplains, to the extent I could put words on what I experienced, and they listened, but a lot of it was beyond what they could hear. I mentioned my sense of vocation to the priesthood, but of course there couldn't be any meeting of the minds. It was just so alien; I might as well have said that I was from Mars.

Depression, breakdown: The calling to priesthood contributed to breaking me open, exposing childhood wounds. In the darkest times I cut myself. The physical pain and the blood-letting were the only release I could find from the inner pain. I took an overdose and was found by one of the chaplains who brought me to Jervis Street hospital to have my stomach pumped. It was brutal. It was a deep cry for help in the midst of overwhelming loneliness, but who could understand my pain?

When the depression got worse I spent some time in St Patrick's psychiatric hospital, which was dark and forbidding. I remember thinking that if one wasn't depressed coming in, one would definitely become depressed in such a gloomy place. Some of my fellow students from Trinity were also being treated there at the same time. One had been in for months and was receiving electroshock therapy. I was terrified the same fate awaited me if I didn't get better.

I had decided to sit the scholarship exams, which meant special examinations in May, and did them while being treated in St Patrick's. An odd situation, but it worked. And while I didn't get a scholarship I passed and was exempted from the September examinations. I would have a free summer, much needed in order to recuperate.

During that second, most difficult college year, I got increasingly involved in the college chaplaincy. Besides attending daily Mass at lunchtime in the chapel, I also got to know the Church of Ireland chaplains, especially the Reverend Cecil Hyland, and I began attending the Anglican

Eucharist which was held in the gallery chapel on Wednesdays. The two celebrations of the Eucharist were held at the same time. Upstairs I could hear the bells below at the time of the Consecration. The scandal of Christian division couldn't have been clearer to me: Two groups of Christians celebrating Eucharist at different tables, at the same time, in the same chapel. I made the decision to accept the hospitality of the Anglicans and to receive Communion.

I also started attending the Anglican evening prayer in the college chapel and got on the rota for reading. They were very courteous and nobody complained, but I must have mispronounced a fair few words of the beautiful English texts. I was grateful to have this opportunity to pray aloud publicly.

At Mass I became an altar server, as several students, males and females, took on the role. Of course female altar servers weren't allowed officially, but the Catholic chaplains weren't going to discriminate. The only issue was when there was an important cleric attending, in which case we had to stay back and let a male near the altar. It was a painful reminder we were not quite the same thing.

I also became unofficial sacristan which meant I had a key to cupboard Number 3 in the sacristy, which was where the Roman Catholics kept their vestments and liturgical gear. I did it until the end of my degree.

My ecumenical involvement also meant that one of my history professors, Professor Moody, a Quaker, asked me to volunteer and visit a Quaker retirement home, Auburn House. Officially I was calling on the elderly residents every fortnight to collect their rent in cash, but actually it was a social call, to have a chat to see if they were all right or needed something. The old people seemed quite happy to have me entertaining them with whatever bits of chat I could provide, and it was a grounding diversion from my inner tribulations.

Looking back on that most painful year, what still astounds me is that I never doubted that calling to the priesthood. Yes, it was profoundly disturbing; yes, I didn't know what to do with it; yes it was agonising; but to me it was very real. So real I couldn't dismiss it. I would have to incorporate that call. It was part of me.

But how? First I had to overcome the depression dragging me down. I would have to learn to live with that calling, as best as I could, a secret very few would know about.

ಬ ಬ ಬ

I DIDN'T SHARE ANY OF THIS WITH my family back in France. I knew they wouldn't understand and would also be very alarmed, or rather further alarmed. They were already disturbed by what they saw on their television screens about Ireland. The violence in the North had become widespread. I tried to reassure them, saying it wasn't in the part of Ireland where I was, but the Troubles had spilled over into the Republic. The bombings in Monaghan and Dublin on 17 May 1974 claimed the lives of 34 men, women and children and 300 people were injured, some horrifically. One of the bombs had been near the railings of Trinity College. With the telephone lines unable to cope with all the frantic calls, it had been several hours before I could call my father to reassure him I wasn't the young French woman student who had been reported killed. I was alive and uninjured, but like all around me aware it could happen again any time, and any of us could be left dead or maimed.

So I never told my family about my mental and spiritual distress, about needing psychiatric care. It was a case of 'what happens in Dublin stays in Dublin'. All they knew was that I seemed to be more religious but was passing all my exams and progressing academically. So I withheld any mention of my small troubles: It was enough that Ireland had become associated with its bloody Troubles.

ଓ ଓ ଓ

AVID READER THAT I WAS I WENT looking for books which could help me understand what I was experiencing in my spiritual life. There were some in the chaplaincy room, but I wanted more. In Eason's I found one from the US which had what I thought was a promising title: *Maturing the Spirit* by Dominic Hoffmann OP. It was subtitled *A Continuation of Spiritual Growth for Contemporary Men and Women* and published in 1973 so I reckoned it would be modern in its outlook. Alas, it contained the same old bias about celibacy and religious life being superior to marriage, and that women, the weaker sex, needed men to guide them spiritually. It was confusing and disappointing.

I was more encouraged when I bought *Friendship in the Lord* by another American Dominican, Paul Hinnebusch. It introduced me to some of the mystics and their friendships across genders. There was more equality and reciprocity.

Back in France on holidays I started making regular trips to La Procure, a large religious bookshop in Paris. I spent hours browsing before spending a large chunk of my student's money there. I discovered Thomas Merton's spiritual autobiography, *Seven Storey Mountain*. Its French title, *La Nuit Privée d'Etoiles* (*The Night Deprived of Stars*), resonated powerfully with me. I too was in a very dark night at sea with no star to guide me. After that I developed a spiritual connection with him and went on to read most of his books.

Then one day in 1975 a bright star rose up in my dark sky. I found the book which gave me the validation I needed: *La Femme, Anti-féminisme et Christianisme* (*Woman, Anti-Feminism and Christianity*), by Jean-Marie Aubert. The author, a respected priest and theologian, showed that the exclusion of women from ordination was not theological but cultural. As patriarchal beliefs gave way to ones where women's subordination was replaced by equality, it would change.

It was the first time I had seen an external confirmation of what I had experienced and come to believe. It was an answer to my prayers: I wasn't the only one who believed women could be priests! All these years later I can still remember the sheer relief I felt as I read it back in my childhood bedroom: 'Yes, and yes, it's only a matter of time.'

But notice that they were all books written by men. Where were the women? Still invisible and voiceless. Like me.

I did, however, make an effort to speak. I gave a talk based on J. M. Aubert's book at the Laurentian Society (a college society for Catholics). There was polite applause from my friends, but it was clear it was not a burning issue for anybody else. I was on my own.

※ ※ ※

WHILE IN TRINITY I WAS INTRODUCED to the unique place that is St Patrick's Purgatory in Lough Derg. One summer I joined a group of students led by the college chaplain,

Brendan Heffernan. It was an adventure and a novelty: the fasting, the long drive on the coach, crossing the border, taking the boat onto the island, the bare feet, endless rosary prayers circling round the stony 'beds', the vigil night trying to keep awake, the salt and pepper soup (hot water!), the midges feasting on us and the solemn renouncing of the 'flesh, the world and the devil'.

That austere, ascetic spirituality was certainly exotic. Trying to describe the three days' pilgrimage and its pious exercises when I was back in France was difficult and met with total incredulity: Doing what? Why?

I went back a second time which was a mistake, or perhaps not. While on the island I got terrible menstrual pain which had me bent in two. I sought permission to lie down indoors but was turfed out mercilessly into the cold. That lack of compassion did it for me: What kind of religion was all hardship and no mercy?

Two decades later I decided to make my peace with Lough Derg, as that experience still rankled with me. I went back with a group of people I didn't know, but I had a very good time. I took nothing too seriously, the facilities had vastly improved and I came home much lighter, having shed my burden of resentment. That being said, I never had a desire to return, despite a friend looking for volunteers to accompany her every summer. The one thing I liked in Lough Derg was the sense of radical equality which prevailed among all us barefoot people.

૪૭ ૪૭ ૪૭

I WAS BACK AT HOME FOR THE SUMMER holidays when my friend Pascaline called me. She had to study for repeat exams in September so asked if I could take her place on a walk/pilgrimage to Italy with her parish youth group? It was a bit daunting because I knew none of them, but I decided I would go. I arranged to meet the priest leading the group and was upfront with him that I was recovering from a nervous breakdown and still fragile.

On the train to Bologna I met the others, half a dozen boys and girls in their late teens. They were fun and accepted me. I soon realised that it was a religious-lite pilgrimage for them, but they respected my spiritual needs.

We walked the 200 kilometres from Bologna to Assisi, pitching our tents at night near small towns. The priest, Roger, about twice our age, was friendly but reserved. I joined him every morning for Mass in the open air as the others were still asleep. We would sit on the ground, a small upturned vegetable crate between us as an altar. We consumed the local bread and wine for Communion. It provided healing and nourishment for my soul.

We climbed up to the sanctuary of La Verna, where St Francis received the stigmata. I remember standing in the cave, aware that something special had happened there, and then finally onto Assisi. I knew a little bit about Francis, but in Assisi he became real to me, a man of flesh and blood. We spent a few days in Assisi, which enchanted me immediately. I got to know an Italian Salesian priest, Gianni, who spoke French and with whom I shared some of my spiritual travails and turmoil. I remember him quoting to me Jesus in the Gospel addressing his disciples who feared drowning: 'O ye of little faith.' After that we kept up a correspondence for a few years.

Besides St Francis, I also became acquainted with St Claire, about whom I knew even less. We visited San Damiano, the convent where she had lived. There a sister gave us a talk about religious life. I was impressed by her faith which was alive and shone through. I could sense her closeness to God and her happiness as a nun. But at the same time I knew it was her vocation, not mine. This came to me with clarity, and it didn't leave me.

From Assisi we took the train to Rome. It was a Holy Year and the city was filled with pilgrims and tourists. While Assisi had been a spiritual oasis, I found little of it in Rome. It certainly didn't help that my long blond hair attracted the attention of the local men who couldn't keep their hands to themselves.

We went to the Vatican. St Peter's was impressive in the way it reminded me of the palace of Versailles in the shadow of which I had grown up. Both had been designed to impress. But in my eyes, it lacked the simplicity, the humility of Assisi. There I had felt at home.

Did we see Pope Paul VI? If we did, it left no impression on me. I bought a Crucifix for the portable altar in Trinity Chapel and sent a postcard to the chaplains with words to that effect: Handsome Swiss guards in Rome but my heart is in Assisi! I came back revived and strengthened.

ဢ ဢ ဢ

ONE SMALL INCIDENT, A VERY BRIEF exchange, has stayed vividly with me from my college days. I was talking with Eamonn McCarthy, one of the chaplains in Trinity, when in front of the Old Library we met Brendan Kennelly, the well known poet and professor of English. We stopped as he and Eamonn exchanged greetings. Then, out of the blue, he turned to me and, pointing at the small Celtic cross around my neck, asked: 'Is he your boyfriend?'

He had a big grin and a slightly mocking tone. I had never previously talked to Brendan Kennelly who was more than twice my age. I only knew him by reputation and was taken aback by his question. How do you answer that? I blushed. He seemed to enjoy my confusion. We went on our way but that question, said in jest, had lodged itself in my mind. 'Was Jesus my boyfriend?'

Well, of course, not. What a ridiculous question! I had boyfriends. Christ was not my boyfriend. It wasn't that kind of relationship. But . . .

Fifty years later I wonder how I would answer Brendan Kennelly now? Yes, it was a love relationship. Christ had captured my heart. Simple as that.

ʚɞ   ʚɞ   ʚɞ

IN OCTOBER 1976 THERE WAS BAD news from Rome. Well, it was bad but hardly news. The Sacred Congregation for the Doctrine of the Faith released a declaration On the Question of Admission of Women to the Ministerial Priesthood (Inter Insigniores). It reaffirmed the exclusion of women from the priesthood. Apparently I was not the only woman who thought she had a vocation to that ministry: It was acknowledged that there were many like me, but we were all deluded, completely misguided in our beliefs.

> It is sometimes said and written in books and periodicals that some women feel that they have a vocation to the priesthood. Such an attraction however noble and understandable, still does not

suffice for a genuine vocation. In fact a vocation cannot be reduced to a mere personal attraction, which can remain purely subjective. Since the priesthood is a particular ministry of which the Church has received the charge and the control, authentication by the Church is indispensable here and is a constitutive part of the vocation: Christ chose 'those he wanted' (Mark 3:13).

And obviously women were not 'those he wanted', then and now. Countless other women like myself around the world were just imagining Christ had chosen us for that ministry. Christ only wanted men, according to churchmen who, after all, were the chosen ones so they knew! There was also a note of warning:

> The roles [in the church] are distinct, and must not be confused; they do not favour the superiority of some vis-a-vis the others, nor do they provide an excuse for jealousy; the only better gift, which can and must be desired, is love (1 Cor 12-13).

So beware of jealous women!

How many women had they actually met and listened to? Again, they didn't need to, they already knew. To do so they had to ignore the findings of their own Pontifical Biblical Commission which a year earlier in 1975 had concluded after an in depth study that the ordination of women could not be ruled out on the basis of scripture. The Commission's report was never published (but was leaked) and its findings have been ignored by the Vatican ever since. Women had been knocking at the door, and instead of opening it we were told to stop knocking, that the door would remain closed to us.

It was a painful blow. Whatever hope of change in the near future was dashed. However, the Declaration failed to convince me, no matter the arguments it made to buttress its claim. But there was nothing I could do. I resigned myself that I wouldn't be able to live that vocation. I would have to find another way to serve. I was in the last year of my degree. I started investigating the possibility of becoming a lay missionary and I joined Viatores Christi, but eventually it became clear that a degree in history and politics would be of no practical use, so that was out. What was I going to do? I was at another crossroads and had to make a decision.

'Why don't you do an MBA?' Eamonn McCarthy suggested. He was being eminently practical: 'It will help you to get a job'. I had never dreamt of a career as a business woman, but I had to concede it was more realistic than this impossible dream of a priestly vocation. So I enrolled on the MBA course in Trinity. Another very challenging year of intense study: At 21 I was the youngest student and only woman in the class of 13; I nearly ran out of the classroom on the first day!

I got my MBA, but even better, I fell in love with a fellow student, Colm Holmes, and a year later we were engaged.

ಬ   ಬ   ಬ

WHEN POPE JOHN PAUL II CAME to Ireland in 1979, the first visit by a pope to this country, I joined in the celebrations. Pope John Paul II had just been elected the year before upon the death of John Paul I, who had died a mere 33 days in office. There was great excitement and many volunteers were called on to help.

I volunteered as a steward for the Mass in the Phoenix Park. Very early on the Saturday morning, while it was still dark, I drove into the Phoenix Park, parked the car and reported for duty. It was going to be a long day for what turned out to be the largest gathering in the state, well over a million people. We were blessed with good weather on this Autumn day.

While I was there, I actually saw very little of the pope, beyond seeing his helicopter's arrival and being greeted by the crowd with a great clamour as if he was the Messiah. While I was happy to help, there was an element of excessive adulation which didn't resonate with me.

I had not grown up with portraits of popes in our home, with papal blessings for weddings and so on, and my trip to Rome four years previously hadn't made a 'papalist' out of me, and of course there was this awkward issue of 'no women priests'.

We were 'corralled' far from the altar so all I could see over the throng of people was the very tall cross which had been erected for the occasion. I was on duty near the toilet block and spent my time looking after children who couldn't find their way back to their parents. Talk about looking after the lost children of Israel, or rather Ireland!

Of course with hindsight I shudder at how none of us stewards had been vetted, as safeguarding concerns hadn't yet surfaced in society, especially in the Church.

Afterwards there was the slow journey back home with my fiancé Colm and his grandmother, Martha, then in her eighties. I was exhausted but glad I had taken an active part. Of course, I didn't know then that Pope John Paul II would reign for 26 years and that his long pontificate would have a major impact on my life.

கு கு கு

THE FIRST PRESENT COLM HAD GIVEN ME was a beautifully decorated egg from India at Christmas 1977. So it was very fitting that we sealed our love on Easter Monday 1980, when Easter eggs were all around. Our wedding invitations spoke of the joy of the Resurrection. We got married in France in a small romanesque church in the wooded countryside beside Port Royal. My parish church would not accept any weddings on that day, but St Lambert des Bois, linked to a Benedictine monastery, welcomed us. Eamonn McCarthy officiated at the Mass in English and French.

I had chosen for the wedding march 'Jesu, Joy of Man's (Woman's!) Desiring' very specially for what its title expressed. My heart had been 'captured' at Easter time in 1974, and so it remained. My love for Colm was part of it, not in competition.

Besides the readings from scripture we had included one by Khalil Gibran 'On Marriage' from *The Prophet*: 'Give your hearts, but not onto each other's keeping, For only the hand of Life can contain your hearts.'

I wore a dress made in West Belfast by my friend Éibhlís Nic Uaithuas's mother, and we prayed for peace in Northern Ireland. As I walked up the aisle, my gold Celtic cross at my neck, I knew the reality of what was inscribed above the church door: '*Lorsque vous êtes réunis en mon nom je suis au milieu de vous*' ('When you are gathered in my name I am in your midst').

Ahead of me toddled my little flower girl, Laetitia (Joy in Latin). I was overflowing with joy as we emerged into the spring sunshine after the final hymn, 'Ave Maria' by Schubert was sung. Yes, Rejoice daughter of Sion, the Holy One is in your midst.

ಬ ಬ ಬ

I WAS NOW HAPPILY SETTLING IN OUR new home in Rathfarnham. After so many moves to student accommodations, I could finally store my small blue steel trunk in the attic.

Beside being married to a man I dearly loved, and who loved me, I had embarked on what looked like the beginning of a brilliant career. Dr Ivor Kenny, director of the Irish Management Institute, certainly thought so. Upon conferring me with a prize for my MBA he had commented: '

> I am particularly fascinated by the subjects she chose for her BA in History & politics, a very intensive study of both Martin Luther and Machiavelli. If she takes a management job in Ireland and applies the philosophies of protest and power as prescribed by the two gentlemen mentioned, she should be very successful indeed in industrial relations.

Less than a year in my first job in a Unilever company, McDonnells, I was recruited by a large firm of accountants and management consultants, Stokes Kennedy Crowley. While working in marketing, I also studied in the College of Industrial Relations, taking the examinations for membership of the Institute of Personnel Management. For a few short years it looked like Ivor Kenny had been prescient.

But no.

As time went on I found myself increasingly at odds with the deepest part of me. I wasn't an ambitious business woman; I couldn't play that role. My heart wasn't in it and slowly it became clear that not only was I in the wrong job, I was in the wrong line of work. I was set on a life path which wasn't mine. Eventually, I made the only decision I could make: At the end of the summer in 1981 I handed in my notice. I was throwing away not just a good job and salary but a management career with good prospects, something I had studied and worked hard for.

I went back to study in September 1981, but this time in University College Dublin (UCD) in Belfield. I enrolled full time in the Diploma in Career Guidance (DCG) and at night over two years I studied for the Diploma in Catechetics. I enjoyed both courses, especially the one in catechetics. It was my first formal theological study as an adult, at a time when there were few opportunities for lay people. As far as I can remember all the lecturers were male clerics. Donal Murray lectured us in moral theology until he was ordained as an auxiliary bishop for Dublin.

It's there that I first heard Alfred Loisy's famous sentence, which has stayed with me ever since: 'Jesus announced the kingdom, and it is the Church that came.' Loisy had been excommunicated as a Modernist heretic, but notwithstanding my own questioning I passed all the exams and even got a prize!

After that I was accepted for the Master's in the Irish School of Ecumenics (ISE). I was in my element studying ecumenical theology and the study of other faiths. I found both the course and the encounters with lecturers and fellow students from diverse backgrounds very stimulating.

I chose for my Master's dissertation 'The God of Hope', an analysis of the work of Jürgen Molltmann, and specialised in Jewish-Christian dialogue with Rabbi Rosen. I felt very much at home in the Irish School of Ecumenics.

After graduation, though, there were very limited openings in terms of ministry for someone like me, who was a Catholic but not a cleric or religious sister.

I decided to volunteer as a counsellor in the Catholic Marriage Advisory Council (CMAC, now ACCORD). I had some counselling training from my DCG course, and in any case training would be supplied. At the initial interview the priest on the panel asked me what I thought about the Church in Ireland. I took a deep breath and told him that I thought the Irish Church was very clericalised, took the people for granted and felt that they would always be there in packed churches. That's how it appeared to my French eyes in 1987. There was silence on the panel and I thought, that's the end of my application. But in fairness to them, I was accepted and received good training, after which I started doing both counselling and also giving inputs in pre-marriage courses.

While a member of the St. Vincent de Paul Society in Trinity College I had already come into contact with the widespread and shocking reality of 'deserted wives', as described in social welfare terminology. Now the counselling of couples or individual marriage partners was a further eye opener into the reality of some people's married lives, including very dark aspects like domestic sexual, physical and emotional violence, controlling behaviour and so on.

I came to the conclusion that some marriages had died, if they ever really existed, and that reconciliation wasn't always possible. Indeed, in some cases the life-saving option was a separation. I was appalled by the prevailing attitude, 'Now you have made your bed, you must lie in it' which, to me, lacked all compassion and condemned many to a life of absolute misery. I couldn't see the God I believed in endorsing that.

The other issue was the official Church position on sexuality and contraception espoused in *Humanae Vitae*, with which I disagreed strongly in conscience. I therefore refused to present and facilitate the sexuality module of the pre-marriage course. I wasn't the only one to opt out for that reason.

On the other hand, I couldn't understand why the module on the spirituality of marriage as a sacrament had to be delivered only by a priest, a celibate man. It seemed particularly incongruous since the couple are the ministers of the sacrament. Obviously, it was presumed that married laypeople were somehow lacking in terms of theology and spirituality. I found that exclusion absurd, irksome and painful.

I also couldn't understand why the director had to be a priest? Were there not plenty of qualified and competent lay people for that role? Why did clerics have to be in charge of everything? Could lay people not be trusted?

I was once called to give witness to the diocese's marriage tribunal, and while it went smoothly, again I wondered why there were only male celibate clerics on it. I wasn't familiar then with the words 'clerical patriarchy', but I certainly was aware of its controlling omnipresence. What I did not know at the time was that two of the judges on the tribunal were child sexual abusers. This was known to the Church authorities, but kept hidden from us.

Ireland's Call and God's Call

It is during these years that I became a mother, first with Killian in 1982 and then Jonathan in 1984. The profound experiences of love-making, pregnancy, labour and giving birth, breast feeding and parenting transformed me. I found though that there was little theological and spiritual reflection on what I was living, in fact a lot of spirituality was quite disembodied. I was fortunate a classmate in the ISE lent me a book by Margaret Hebblethwaite, *Motherhood and God*, which was published the year our second son was born. That ground-breaking book confirmed what I was experiencing. After reading so many books by male theologians, this was the first spiritual book I had read by a woman.

Soon after the birth of our second child I had been moved to write a poem about it as a glimpse of the Mystery of the Incarnation. I never wrote poems, so that was unusual, but I had to try to put it into words. I sent it to the Irish Childbirth Trust who published it in their newsletter, and later to *Reality*, the Redemptorist Magazine. The poem is entitled 'Jonathan Emmanuel':

> Your father and I were one in love and you became.
> Nine months in the secret of my womb I carried you,
> Your heart beating – a little faster – beneath mine,
> Your hidden presence more and more visible as
> Your growing body stretched mine to its fullness,
> Your first move – like a fluttering butterfly – filled me with
>   joyful praise,
> Your dancing made me glad,
> I ached from your thumping and tossing but your
>   stillness made me anxious.

A Divine Calling

Your father fondled you through my skin,
   we talked to you,
Making up imaginary answers.
You were my constant companion with whom I shared
   everything – even exams!
So intimate, so close, and yet a stranger within my own
   flesh,
Your face unknown – a boy or a girl?
You kept us guessing – and we guessed wrong!
As Spring came I grew more and more impatient.
My arms longed to hold you, my breasts to suckle
   you and
My eyes to look into your eyes.
I started counting the weeks and then the days.
It seemed an eternity.
We finally met – so to speak – on a sunny May afternoon,
When your life sprang forth.
The storm that shook my body to its roots and tore it apart
Expelled you from your cosy nest. La Délivrance!
We shared in the same painful drama from which there is
   no going back.
But I wonder: did you also share in that infinite joy
When I held you skin to skin – at last!
That precious moment which I shall for ever treasure,
When time stopped and the broken world was
   made whole again.
I caught a glimpse of the Incarnation and I named you
Jonathan Emmanuel!

(In Hebrew, Jonathan means 'The Lord has given' and Emmanuel means 'God with us')

༄ ༄ ༄

AND WHAT ABOUT THE CALLING to the priesthood which had disturbed me so much? On the morning of our wedding, in the midst of all the last minute preparations, a thought arrived: 'Ordination will come for women sometime in the future, but not for me, because now I am married.'

I had never shared with Colm that sense of vocation. What would have been the point? It was unachievable. As far as I was concerned my marriage had put an end to it. I was at peace with it, I thought, and I would live my faith to the full as a married lay person. For ten years this is what I did and any sense of vocation to the priesthood was left behind. It would only briefly re-surface on a few occasions, but then it would recede and be forgotten.

On the annual Good Shepherd Sundays when at Mass there were appeals for men to come forward it was like a stab to my heart, but it would quickly pass. Apart from these direct reminders, there was one other occasion I remember well. While in the ISE I was told there was a French Jesuit priest who was a bit homesick and who would be glad of a chat in French. I agreed to meet him, and we had a very pleasant conversation about all kinds of topics, nothing specific about priesthood. At some stage, though, while we were chatting, I thought, 'I have the same vocation as him'. I registered the thought, but then let it go. What else could I do with it?

But when our eldest son Killian, preparing for his First Holy Communion, announced that women could not be priests, I was jolted into telling him that this was wrong and it would change. I was shocked and wondered how many more generations would be indoctrinated with this sexist belief?

3.

The Lord's Year of Favour

The year 1990 remains an exceptional one, a turning point, even though no major event took place, externally that is. What happened was all largely in my inner life.

I have sometimes described it as a rumbling volcano, finally erupting, or the labour contractions of birthing. These are just metaphors to convey the sense of an inner process over which I had no control. At times it felt like being on a roller coaster and a mystery train all at once, hurtling towards an unknown destination. Whatever was at work within me was active and powerful.

'Trust the process' was the repeated advice from Maureen, a wise friend in CMAC to whom I confided, and she recommended a book by William Johnston SJ, *Being in Love: The Practice of Christian Prayer*. It was indeed helpful, which I was able to convey to the author himself years later when I met him on one of his trips home from Japan.

One Saturday I was attending a session for members of the Teams of Our Lady in Killiney when, for some reason, I felt the desire to go to confession. I decided to go to Eamonn McCarthy, the former chaplain in Trinity, who was now a curate in Ballybrack. I called to his home, made my confession, had a chat with him and went home.

That evening I experienced something like a gentle wind on the embers in my heart and a fire being rekindled. That was only a beginning, but still I was aware something had shifted.

After that, I started weeping, weeping as I had never done before or since. I have cried many times in my life, but this was truly different. It went on for weeks, with very little pause. It wasn't sobbing, it was just quiet, ongoing, weeping. What would have I said if somebody had asked me why I was crying? I wouldn't have been able to explain it: there was no illness, no bereavement or loss. It was like a tap had been opened and the water just flowed.

At the same time, buried emotions and memories started surfacing. It got worse and I wondered whether I was disintegrating, coming apart. I remembered my mental struggles while in college and wondered whether I was heading for another breakdown. What was happening to me? I feared having to go back to a psychiatric hospital. I now had two children who needed me; I clung on to my sanity. I confided in Eamonn McCarthy, who agreed to accompany me spiritually, although it was all rather bewildering.

As the months passed, I remember crying out in anguish: 'I am thirt-three and I still haven't done anything for Christ!' There was a fierce spiritual struggle going on within me. For a time I couldn't look at a crucifix, couldn't even make the sign of the cross. I would recoil, literally sick with fear.

Then there were moments of pure ecstasy. I never knew when they would happen, or for how long. I certainly couldn't make them happen or stop. Sometimes I would be filled with such a delightful sweetness, I could taste honey in my mouth. At other times I felt myself held in a strong loving embrace.

In counterpoint there were times of dreadful agony. I was familiar with pain and despair, but this was to a degree which was previously unknown to me. At times I was plunged into complete darkness. Once I experienced what felt like absolute nothingness. It lasted only a few hours but seemed unbearably long.

It was like straddling two worlds. The world of the mundane, the domestic tasks, collecting the boys at school, where nothing had changed, and the spiritual world where everything was upside down and utterly changed. I had left the harbour and lost sight of the shore. All I could do was to 'trust the process'.

On this strange journey I reached a stage where I no longer knew who I was. I still knew when and where I was born, who my parents were, who I was married to etc. but these were just biographical data. Somehow I was detached from them, they were meaningless.

They didn't answer the question which was now arising in me. Who am I? The question was so real, so urgent, I thought of phoning Colm at work to ask him, but the rational part of me knew it wasn't a simple question of identity. And then the answer arose effortlessly from the depths, 'You are the Christ, the Son of the Living God', and the question fell away. I was left in wonder.

Throughout this I was going daily to Mass in Ballybrack and sharing with Eamonn all that was happening inside me. A lot of it was difficult to express in words, but at least here was a person who knew me since my teenage years, who knew my spiritual journey, who was my confessor,

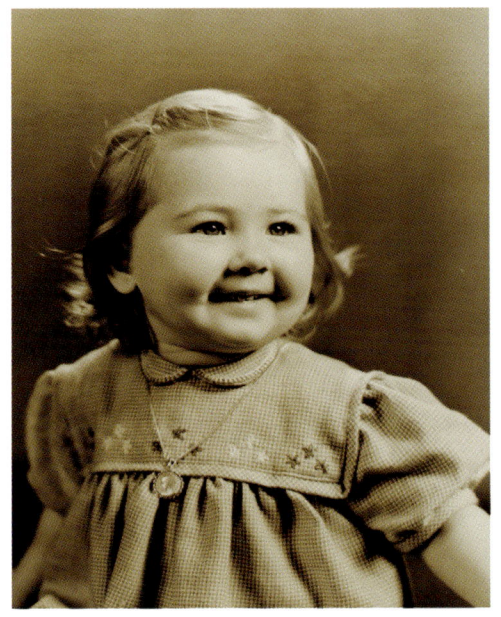
Here I am!

With two doves . . . à la St Francis

With my father at the Palace of Versailles

With my mother and brother Didier

My mother's last summer

Profession of Faith

Teenager

Last year at school

Graduation with Colm Holmes, Eamon McCarthy and René Vatinel

Our wedding day in France

With sons Killian and Jonathan in the Irish Press

At the NCPI Conference with Archbishop Seán Brady, Hannah O'Brien and Pat O'Brien

Basilica of St Marie-Madeleine, St Maximin-la-St Baume with RTÉ

New alb and stole

With Mary McAleese and Professor Enda McDonagh presenting BASIC book to President Mary Robinson in Áras an Uachtaráin

First World Day of Prayer for Women's Ordination, 1994, outside the GPO in Dublin

One of many protest/prayer vigils outside the Dublin Nunciature – Jubilee Year 2000

Protest at the Nunciature

and would not dismiss what was happening to me as fantasy or insanity. That was a precious gift.

As weeks passed, I did not know what would become of me. In early autumn I eventually found myself able to say that 'yes' that I had been struggling with. Not for the first time, it happened in the midst of the most mundane task: I had my hands in the sink, washing glasses, when I felt a wholehearted 'yes' to something, or more accurately, Somebody, a 'yes' from my whole being, and it brought me great peace.

As St Paul wrote to the Philippians 3:8-14:

> Indeed, I count everything as loss, because of the surpassing worth of knowing Christ Jesus my Lord. For his sake I have suffered the loss of all things and count them as rubbish, in order that I may gain Christ and be found in Him.

Then there was the light when everything was lit up. It was so dazzling I could hardly keep my eyes open. It lasted a few days then it faded away. It all seems quite incredible now, but yet this experience is indelibly etched in my mind. To have seen the world illuminated in such a way filled me with joy, with love, with sweet peace.

Another experience which I cannot forget happened while I was shopping for dinner. I suddenly found myself, for no reason whatsoever, filled with laughter in the depths of my being. No sound passed my lips. It was a silent laughter deep inside me, silent but very powerful. I somehow understood it was the Holy Spirit which filled me with joy.

During these months one sentence from scripture came to me in prayer, which I remember clearly. Jesus asks his disciples, 'Can you drink the cup I shall drink?' To that same question addressed to me all I could reply was, 'No, I can't, but with your grace I will'.

In late August I had a *nuit de feu*, a night of fire. As Colm and the children were asleep, I felt impelled to go down to sit at the table. There I stayed most of the night, completely still, wide awake, very calm and peaceful, captivated by a Presence that was invisible but no less real. As morning came I finally stirred. I was thoroughly refreshed, even though I had not slept at all. Later I told Eamonn McCarthy it had been like a wedding night, a spiritual union.

ಐ ಐ ಐ

IN THESE MONTHS OF 1990, I HAD been taken into a dark space where I was completely disorientated. Strange as it may seem, it was the account of a man who had been held hostage for years which resonated most with my experience. Brian Keenan, a Belfast man, had been kidnapped in 1986 in Lebanon and was released in August 1990. He gave a powerfully moving press conference in Dublin in which he described his ordeal. The account by Andy Pollak in *The Irish Times* of 31 August resonated with my own plight at the time.

> What is a hostage? A hostage is crucifying aloneness. There is silent, screaming slide into the bowels of ultimate despair. A hostage is a man hanging by his fingernails over the edge of chaos and feeling his fingers slowly straightening. A hostage is the humiliating stripping away of every sense and fibre of body and mind and spirit that make you what you are. A hostage is a mutant creation, full of self-

loathing, guilt and death-wishing. But he is a man – a rare, unique and beautiful creation of which these things are no part.

How could I possibly identify with Brian Keenan, when I had not been physically captive in harsh conditions as he had? The reality was that somehow, in the depths of my being, I had experienced being a hostage, powerless in captivity until eventually released and transformed. In my own way, I too had been in hell in my spirit.

Brian Keenan wrote about this captivity in a book, *An Evil Cradling*. Colm bought me a copy and I put the *Irish Times* article inside it, where it still is. In the preface, Brian Keenan writes:

> A zealous poet might describe the experience as a deification of one's humanity. In the most intense moments of despair and suffering, something of this was truly present.

ꙮ ꙮ ꙮ

AUTUMN HAD ARRIVED AND with it came the long buried memory of an episode in Trinity College. It suddenly surfaced, much to my surprise, as I had completely forgotten about it. What prompted it and why now? Just one more mystery, but by then I was up to my neck in mystery.

The scene was well preserved in my memory, even though it had happened fourteen years previously. It was September 1976, I was in third year studying for my history exams in Trinity College. There were only a small number of students around as the college year would only really start in October. All was very quiet.

I had rooms upstairs in the old part of the college in Front Square, which consisted of a main room and bedroom, and across from the landing a kitchenette.

One day in my kitchenette I was startled by a man suddenly appearing at the door I had left open. I hadn't heard him climbing up the stone stairs. I was aware there had been sexual attacks on campus and we had been warned to be vigilant. But here he was, asking me for something to eat. I replied I could give him bread and strawberry jam, which was all I had. Would he take a sandwich? He said yes, but could he sit and have it with me? I agreed, realising I was taking another risk.

Back in my main room I cleared my textbooks from the table and we sat down to eat bread and jam and drink hot chocolate. He was a pleasant, dark haired young man. I say young but he was probably about thirty, while I was just twenty. I do not remember our conversation, except for him telling me he was the eldest of many brothers and sisters and he looked after them.

Then, for some reason I cannot explain, I went to my bedroom (another risk) to get a rosary ring I had. It was a plain metal ring, hanging on a leather tong, which I had since my scout days in France, and with which I had prayed in Lough Derg when on pilgrimage with the college chaplain. It had no monetary value, but I was attached to it.

Anyway, whatever possessed me, I handed it over to the stranger. Why? Surely some cash would have made more sense. But lo and behold, the young man beamed with joy when I gave him my rosary ring as if it was a great treasure and promptly put it around his neck. He thanked me and left. I cleared up the plates, went back to my studies and put it all behind me. After all, nothing had happened.

I had completely forgotten about this incident until the souvenir of this brief encounter suddenly reappeared. On 14 October, Eamonn went on a priests' retreat in Tabor House in Milltown for a week. I kept going to daily Mass in the parish, and one day as I was leaving a parishioner approached me, holding up a rosary ring: 'Is this yours?' After weeks of wondering what had become of my rosary ring, I was amazed. I saw it as an answer, said yes, and took it.

I felt I had to share this providential find with Eamonn. I drove to Milltown and went into Tabor House looking for him. The receptionist told me the priests were about to celebrate Mass at midday. I climbed up the stairs and saw a Jesuit priest outside the retreat room putting on vestments. I asked if I could join in. He was very reluctant but Eamonn prevailed to let me in. There were a dozen priests sitting around the room for the liturgy. They must have wondered what on earth this woman was doing barging in during their diocesan retreat.

After the Gospel there was a pause for sharing. I was moved to open the Bible which was at the page in Luke's gospel where Jesus is in the synagogue in Nazareth, and I read out, 'The Spirit of the Lord is upon me, he has anointed me and sent me to proclaim good news.' Silence followed. Nobody said a word.

Then the Eucharistic prayer was read and all the priests, together with the presider, extended their hands at the consecration. At that moment, I also extended my hand. It was a very deliberate gesture. I was one of them, with the same ministry. The calling I had first 'heard' when I was seventeen and which I had put behind me as 'impossible', had now been 'fulfilled today in your hearing'. It was a revelation to me, so powerful that it has shaped my life since: I am a priest (presbyter). As we prayed the Our Father we held hands. My own hands were throbbing so strongly it was as if my heart was in them.

The Rosary, given to that mysterious stranger who had come to 'eat and drink supper' with me all these years ago, had led to this other Eucharist. I have shared this with very few, and it is only now that I record it in writing.

My sense of wonder at these events has not diminished with the passage of time. Quite the contrary, as I look back their decisive significance appears even more clearly. They unfolded in a way which remains filled with the mysterious presence and action of the Holy Spirit. When I left Tabor House in Milltown on that day in October I was set on a new path in the footsteps of the One who had called me.

As the liturgical reading on that day proclaimed: 'Glory be to God, whose power working in us can do infinitely more than we can ask or imagine' (Ephesians 3:20). It definitely had been beyond my wildest imaginings.

℘ ℘ ℘

NOBODY WAS MORE SURPRISED THAN I was that this calling to the priesthood had returned, loud and clear, summoning me to respond, 'Here I am'. This time I was open to it. I did not pray, 'Do not call me, your church doesn't want me'. Together with Mary's great 'Yes' at the Annunciation, I said my own little 'Yes'. There was no struggle, just peace and joy.

But as I lay awake in bed, I did wonder, 'How will it come about? I am still a woman and now I am married and I have two children and your church has not changed.' Reasonable questions.

The answer I got was the same one Mary had received: 'The Holy Spirit will bring it about.' There was nothing more to be said. I believed God's word was God's bond. Yes, I was well aware it seemed impossible, but with God nothing is impossible. I rested silently in the mystery all night.

I now had to tell Colm that the calling to the priesthood which I had experienced in my teens had come back. It was quite a challenging reality for him to adjust to – that his wife and mother of two sons had been called to be a Catholic priest – but Colm did. He asked Eamonn what he thought, and Eamonn, having witnessed my spiritual journey since college, confirmed that he believed my calling to be genuine. So that was it. Both these men embarked with me on an adventure which would prove challenging for each of us. But their belief in my vocation and faithful support would never waver.

I had received the divine assurance that 'the Spirit will bring it about'. Somewhat naively at first, I thought that since God was calling women to the presbyteral ministry, God would inform Church leaders of this fact. But it soon dawned on me that it wouldn't happen that way. And I couldn't just wait passively for the pope to have a divine revelation about women priests. I would have to do something about it, but what?

I decided I would be the messenger to tell Church leaders about it. I had to tell them: 'This is what God is doing in my life'. It was Good News and I had to bear witness to it. I would start with asking for a meeting with my local bishop, Bishop Donal Murray. In time I would seek meetings with many others, including the Bishop of Rome. I would soon find out, however, that being the bearer of Good News was no guarantee of a welcome, and indeed would result in quite the opposite.

ಬ ಬ ಬ

BUT THERE WAS SOMEBODY ELSE accompanying me on that path: Saint Francis. As I mentioned earlier, he had been a presence in my life since my pilgrimage to Assisi in 1975.

I had given his name as middle name to our first son in 1982, and when we had moved to Blackrock, County Dublin, I had named our house after him. It was like nailing my colours to the mast.

Now that my life was again being turned upside down, Francis rose up like a lamp to lead the way. In France I had bought a biography of St Francis called *Frère François* by Julien Green. On the dust jacket there was a reproduction of the oldest portrait of the saint from a fresco in Subiaco. Strictly speaking, it is not an icon, but it held my gaze like one. Francis' wide open eyes were like windows into his soul, into the divine. I removed the dust jacket, trimmed the image and framed it for prayer and contemplation.

With Francis came St Claire, and in October 1990 in Tabor House I heard inwardly the same call Francis had heard: 'Repair my Church which has fallen into ruins.'

I saw a poster for the film *The Mission* in the corridor which seemed to reinforce the message.

4.

Brothers and Sisters in Christ

Still filled with enthusiasm and hope at the beginning of 1991, I made an appointment to meet Bishop Donal Murray, my local bishop, to share with him my sense of calling. It was my first venture into a closed hierarchical, clerical, male, celibate world which was completely alien to me. At least with Bishop Murray it was a bit less daunting because he had been my lecturer in moral theology, although I had not met him since he had become the youngest member of the Irish hierarchy nine years previously.

We met for well over an hour, after which I drove home in tears, my enthusiasm and hope in tatters. Donal Murray had received me courteously, but it was clear there was an abyss between us as we were living in two different worlds. I had come bearing what I thought, perhaps naively, was good news for the Church, but for a bishop it was very bad news indeed: It would spell the end of the millennium-old male celibate ordained ministry, a radical change.

In keeping with official theology, Donal Murray informed me it was impossible for me, or any woman, to be a priest. He didn't go into complex sacramental arguments but summarised the reason as such: 'Women cannot be priests, because men don't have children'.

I was flummoxed. I thought: 'But men do have children ... Colm has two children, our two sons, they are as much his as mine.'

Afterwards I realised he had meant to say 'men don't give birth to children', but the way he said it made my jaw drop. Not that I would have been any more impressed if he had framed the argument that other way. I just couldn't see the relevance.

He was adamant: 'A bishop could be laying hands on a woman, nothing would happen.' The reason for this was that woman is not proper matter for the Sacrament of Orders, essentially unfit for the ontological character.

In addition, there must be a natural resemblance between Christ and the minister to act in the person of Christ and only a man (male human being) carries that resemblance to Christ.

I had read all these arguments before so they were not new to me. But I had never heard a bishop address them to me personally, arguing that my sense of calling to the presbyteral ministry was both impossible and misguided, a chimera.

'You have a very Protestant understanding of vocation. It's not the Catholic understanding. It is not God who calls one to the priesthood, it is the Church who does. And the Church is not calling women.'

That also flummoxed me: what about all these Church appeals: 'Do you feel God is calling you to serve his people as a priest?' And there was even this small ad in *The Irish Times* one year:

> We've done this ad just in case you were asleep when you felt the calling.
>
> Information day for people interested in the priesthood for the Dublin Diocese . . .

Note: The ad said 'people', and aren't women people?

No doubt if I had been a young unmarried man who had told Bishop Murray I felt God may be calling me to be a priest I would have been admitted to the seminary for training and discernment, not told this feeling was a Protestant one (now go back to sleep!).

Interestingly, while my bishop was informing me of an ontological inability to be ordained because I lacked 'natural resemblance' to Christ, a little boy had a very different message for me. Jason, not yet three, used to accompany his father to daily Mass; I often sat beside them in the pew.

One day I was in the supermarket when I was startled to hear a little voice crying out: 'Jesus is in the supermarket, Jesus is in the supermarket!' and I saw little Jason sitting on his mother's trolley pointing at me. His mother, equally startled, told him: 'It's Soline, it's Soline.' But Jason persisted that 'Jesus is in the supermarket'. . . And afterwards, whenever I would meet him it would be the same. No matter how often his parents would repeat my name, for little Jason I was always 'Jesus'.

I was rather perplexed by this and mentioned it to the priest of the parish. His answer was that very young children sometimes call the priest 'Jesus'. 'Yes, but Jason doesn't call you Jesus. He calls me Jesus' I replied. There was no rational explanation we could think of. Out of the mouths of babes . . .

A few weeks later I had a similar encounter in another supermarket. As I was shopping a woman approached to speak to me. I could see she was a bit self-conscious as she spoke tentatively. 'Excuse me, I do not know you and I don't know if you're religious, but I want to tell you, you could be Jesus.' Just like that! No wonder the poor woman was hesitant about speaking these words to a perfect stranger.

All I could do was thank her for her kind words. She left relieved, and I continued with more to ponder about that 'natural resemblance between the minister and Christ' I was officially lacking.

So first little Jason and then this woman. How was it they could see what the bishop could not see?

> At that time Jesus said, 'I praise you, Father, Lord of heaven and earth, because you have hidden these things from the wise and learned, and revealed them to little children. Yes, Father, for this was your good pleasure' (Matt 11:25-26).

I was grateful for these encounters, a gift from God, to sustain me in my vocation when the official Church leaders were dismissing it as a figment of my female imagination.

I was only beginning to find out how powerful the opposition actually was.

ಐ ಐ ಐ

THE AUSTRALIAN CARDINAL EDWARD Cassidy, president of the Pontifical Council for the Promotion of Christian Unity, was in Dublin. He had several public engagements linked to having just been 'created' a cardinal and as a graduate of the Irish School of Ecumenics I attended one of them. After the speeches I found myself beside him at some stage in a crowded room, so I plucked up my courage to ask him: 'Why are women not ordained in the Catholic Church?'

In a peremptory, cutting tone he replied, 'Because Jesus said no.'

I dared persist: 'Where does it say, Jesus said no?'

I'll never know the answer because Cardinal Cassidy, mouth pinched, briskly turned on his heels and moved off.

The British Ambassador, Nicholas Fenn, the son of a Presbyterian minister, had overheard our exchange. He had a personal interest in theological matters and empathised with me: 'I am very sorry you got such a response.'

He was not impressed, I was not impressed. I wondered how somebody in charge of ecumenical relations could be so poor at dialogue, but then I was a woman, of no importance, and almost all of the official ecumenical dialogue was amongst male clerics.

It was clearly not his intention, but Cardinal Cassidy left me even more convinced that Jesus never said no!

ಸಿ ಸಿ ಸಿ

WHATEVER ABOUT TELLING CHURCHMEN, the time had come to tell my father about my vocation. How would he react? I chose a moment when he was over on holidays and we were on our own in the kitchen, a quiet moment after a meal. I told him simply how I had first experienced that call in college and how it had re-surfaced, and that I was now pursuing it. He listened intently, without saying a word. If he was surprised, he didn't show it. When I had finished he just said quietly: 'You are going to suffer very much'. That's all.

I was standing at the sink, looking at the garden through the window. His words pierced my heart and have never left me. I knew they were true. I did not want them to be true, but I knew they were. There was a long silence. 'I know,' I finally managed to say. I wanted to tell him there was also joy in this vocation, but I didn't. Was it because I felt he would not understand? The suffering was obvious, but the joy?

ဢ ဢ ဢ

NOW THAT THIS SENSE OF VOCATION had come back and I had said yes to it, I had to decide how I could fulfil it. I figured a first step might be taking the degree course in theology and ministry in the Milltown Institute.

On the first day of the course in September 1991, students were asked by one of the lecturers to introduce themselves and say why they were doing the course. There were some women, but most were young men who said they were in religious life and studying towards ordination to the priesthood. When my turn finally came, I don't remember what reason I gave, but I do know that I did not say I had a vocation to the priesthood. I wanted to because it was the reason I was there, but I could not say it. It stuck in my throat.

I wondered whether I lacked courage or whether I had discerned wisely it wasn't appropriate at that stage. In any case, to this day it feels that I denied part of who I was. After that I resolved that never again would I hide my vocation.

I have always enjoyed studying and had a real hunger for theology, so I was in my element. There was a lot of philosophy which reconnected me with my baccalauréat major. I researched for an extended essay on St Augustine and also did one on homosexuality for the moral theology component. There I first encountered the writings of John J. McNeill SJ.

But in many other ways, and increasingly so, I was *not* in my element: I had studied ecumenical theology which had given me a breadth of vision that I was now missing. Ecumenism was an optional extra subject which interested very few. It wasn't too long before I realised the course might have been suitable for me 10 years earlier, but I couldn't turn back the clock.

The overwhelming number of lecturers were male clerics. Some were good, but many had very narrow views on women. I remember one lecturer pontificating at length on motherhood and stating how children always called for their mother. As one of the very few mothers (if not the only one in that particular class) I felt obliged to interject that at night our sons called for their father.

I also objected when the same lecturer asserted that in sexual matters it was up to the woman to say no to the man. Obviously in his view men had very limited moral agency and responsibility.

Besides patriarchal views I also had to contend with an abundance of clericalism. There was no doubt that lay students were considered by many as being in an inferior category. Many of the young male religious saw themselves set on a higher track than we were. I could see them slowly rising in a lift to the upper floors while looking down at us who remained at ground level, or even in the basement.

In their view celibacy was far superior spiritually: 'We give ourselves 100 per cent to God' one told me. To which

I replied: 'Do you take 50 per cent off for marriage and a further 10 per cent for each child?'

It all started to wear me down. After a few months I began to open up with some of my fellow students about my sense of calling. Not surprisingly, it exposed me to some hostility and ridicule. 'Prove you have a vocation to the priesthood!' One challenged me sarcastically.

'How do you prove you have a vocation?' I replied.

'We don't have to, we are men,' he said smugly. And I was only a woman.

In fairness there were exceptions, both among the staff and the students. A young man who was a Redemptorist novice was very supportive, and comforted me after the worse taunts, saying, 'Don't mind them, they are dinosaurs'.

A lecturer, a Jesuit, once told me: 'Why do you want to be a priest? You are a prophet!' He didn't elaborate but surely it was my vocation which was prophetic? It became increasingly painful, unbearably so.

At home three days before Christmas I took out the children's paint box and painted a woman hanging on a cross. I hadn't painted since primary school and didn't know what my paint brush would produce. But there she was, a young naked woman on a cross. All in black. A stark image. Myself.

I put a caption: *She was not raised from the dead, God forsaken. A woman. Still crucified.*

After Christmas I plucked up the courage and pinned a copy of my Woman on the Cross on the students' notice board in Milltown. It didn't last long. It was swiftly taken down and a notice went up: 'The management is not responsible for the content on the students' notice board.' For years, each time I was in the building passing

through that corridor I smiled on seeing the notice. Who is afraid of a woman on the Cross?

At Easter it became clear to me I would finish the year but wouldn't return for second year. I couldn't breathe in that environment. I had never dropped out of a course I had started so it was a difficult decision. But what made it particularly hard was my belief that I was abandoning the possibility of qualifying for ministry when women's ordination finally did come. But I had to leave, everything within me said to get out.

With the Easter ceremonies I experienced the pain of Church discrimination and exclusion so acutely that I felt I could no longer stay in the Church . It was too oppressive. On April 26 I wrote a letter to Bishop Donal Murray in which I communicated my decision to leave the Church and the reasons for it. I hadn't been baptised into slavery, and yet the way I, a woman, was treated in the Church was one of subjugation under male domination. It had become unbearably injurious to my spirit.

How could I possibly stay in an organisation where women were declared to be equal but in reality were treated as inferior? The more I looked the more appalling the situation was: Centuries of misogyny and sexism were hard-baked into the fabric of the Church and permeating every aspect of it. Where was the liberating Gospel, the Good News, in all this? I posted a copy of the letter on the Milltown notice board where the Woman On the Cross had been taken down.

At the end of June I was shocked to hear that the famous Brazilian Liberation theologian Leonardo Boff had left the Franciscans. He had openly denounced the Congregation for the Doctrine of the Faith (CDF) – formerly the inquisition – for its oppressive methods and denials of human rights. He would not agree to being censured and silenced.

This was the catalyst for my very first letter to *The Irish Times* on the issue of the Ordination of Women. It was published prominently at the top of the page on 6 July. It's worthwhile quoting it in full. (I would go on to have dozens of letters and Rite & Reason articles published in the IT on the subject but this one remains relevant to this day).

Women and the Church (*The Irish Times*, Monday, 6 July 1992)

Sir,

Bishop Brendan Comiskey's statement that the issue of the ordination of women is 'basically an organisational detail and not of the core beliefs of the Church (Irish Times July 1st) appears to be in direct contradiction with the Archbishop of Dublin's statement in last year's Lenten Pastoral: 'The Church has always and everywhere followed the example of Christ, to which Saint Paul refers as a command from the Lord (1Cor.14:37), by calling only men to ordination; and she does not consider herself authorised ever to depart from this practice.'

However I reject both views:

To say that the issue is an organisational detail implies that it is of minor importance and has no moral or dogmatic implications; quite the opposite is true for it challenges in a radical and far reaching way our understanding of God, women and the relationship between men and women, the priesthood and of the Church itself.

Such a statement also sadly displays a remarkable lack of sensitivity to the real suffering of all those who are barred from exercising the ministry of service to which they are called.

What is an 'organisational detail' for Bishop Comiskey is a heavy cross on the shoulders of thousands of women (myself included), and an impoverishment of the whole community.

On the other hand, to affirm, as Archbishop Desmond Connell does, that to ordain women would be to disobey God, begs the question ; Does the Roman Catholic Church witness to a man-made sexist idol constituted in its image to justify its prejudice, or to the Way, the Truth and the Life?

The refusal to ordain women must be clearly seen for what it is: neither an organisational detail nor the Lord's command, but 'one of the most clear examples of the violation of human rights in the Church.' So wrote the Liberation Theologian Leonardo Boff in 'Church, Charisma and Power' (pp 35 and 36). As recent days have shown he has paid a heavy price for speaking on behalf of all the oppressed. But that is the way they have always treated the prophets!

Yours, etc.

Soline Vatinel

The following day, 7 July, I went for a walk on Dun Laoghaire pier. I strolled in the sunshine, pondering the events of the past few months, and when I reached the end of the pier I 'heard' an inner voice. Just one sentence, which cut me to the quick: 'I have bound myself to my Church and I will not leave it, even though it crucifies me'. As I turned around to walk back, I knew I also needed to turn back to the Church. 'The servant is not greater than the Master.' It was my *Quo Vadis* moment, much like Saint Peter leaving Rome during the persecutions but returning after meeting Christ.

So on 12 July I wrote again to Bishop Donal Murray, telling him I had decided to stay in the Church after all! I didn't mention my *Quo Vadis* experience, but that was the reason.

I also applied for ordination. Donal Murray replied, welcoming me back to my spiritual home.

I stayed because of Christ. Nothing else could have kept me in the Church through the following decades with the horrific revelations of corruption, crimes and abuses of all kinds.

☙ ☙ ☙

SUMMER HOLIDAYS IN FRANCE OR elsewhere didn't mean a vacation from what was happening within. Sometimes it even surfaced more strongly. On the outside I may have been looking like I was just leisurely sunbathing on the beach, but inside I was frequently pondering deeper things.

In August 1992 I found myself engaged in a mighty struggle with the Holy Trinity. It wasn't because of the number but because of gender: It wasn't the 'three persons in one mystery', but three persons with a male pronoun. Three times *he*.

While I knew that God had no gender, the male language for the triune God was now blocking me. I was hitting against these male words – father, son, spirit, he, he, he – like a bird hitting repeatedly against a window pane while trying to fly out of a room it has entered by accident.

I felt trapped by that exclusively male language for the divine in which I had bathed all my life. With that male Trinity women like me would always be subordinate, second class, in the Church. A male Trinity buttressed patriarchy. I knew very well the Divine Mystery was beyond gender, but the official and prescribed language was a formidable obstacle. Like Jacob I was wrestling with that angel, on the beach and in bed at night, without finding an issue.

A Divine Calling

One day, a weekday, I went to the local parish church. I had arrived too late for Mass, but the priest was still there and agreed to give me Communion from the tabernacle. I then had a long conversation with him. Not about the Trinity, but about my sense of vocation. He listened attentively and then told me he had heard other women voicing the same sense of vocation, but never with the same strength of conviction as I did. In turn, he confided that following his own vocation had cost him a lot because his father had been opposed to it. He knew pain. He then asked me whether I would like to be a minister of the Eucharist at the Sunday Mass, which I did.

It didn't resolve my Trinity struggle, but it put some balm on the wound. I had met a priest who was a good Samaritan. I do not know exactly how or when I got beyond that male language barrier, but I did. It lost its power over my spirit and no longer imprisoned me.

I had read theology books about it like those by Catherine Mowry LaCugna and Gavin d'Costa, but it couldn't be resolved in the mind. It required a light in my spirit to roll away that stone which shut me in. And that eventually came through grace, not my own efforts.

༄ ༄ ༄

My 'coming out' on the national airwaves was purely accidental, or at least it wasn't planned. But it wasn't premature. I was listening to the News at One on RTÉ Radio 1 on 12 November 1992 when I heard that the Anglican vote for women priests was going to be discussed on the next programme, *Liveline*. I had never phoned a radio programme before but felt impelled to express my joy at that historic vote. All I intended to say was as a Catholic woman I was delighted by that decision.

But I hadn't reckoned with the curiosity of the researcher who listened to me and then asked: 'Why is this so important for you? Are you a nun? Would you want to be a priest?'

'No, I am a married woman, but yes, I have a vocation to the priesthood.'

'Would you be willing to go live on air and speak to Marian Finucane?'

It was too late to back out. I said, 'Yes, but it must be in the next half an hour because I need to collect my children at school.' And so I told Marian Finucane and a large number of listeners about my sense of vocation. It wasn't very long, but it was quite clear and had now been said aloud for everyone to hear.

I arrived at the school gate and noticed the other mothers looking at me with a bemused look on their faces. They had been listening to *Liveline*, and while only my first name had been mentioned there weren't too many Solines with a French accent: I was out!

'Was it you I just heard on the radio?'

'Yes, it was.'

There was no negative reaction, but I sensed a certain puzzlement. There would be no further discussion. I came home with two young sons thankfully oblivious to their mother's strange debut on the airwaves. Another bridge had been crossed.

৪০ ৪০ ৪০

A Divine Calling

IN JANUARY 1993 THE CALL CAME from my father to come home immediately. My grandmother, his mother, was very ill and dying.

I decided to fly to Bordeaux where she lived with my aunt and booked a ticket for a week. Before I went I asked Eamonn to give me a pyx with consecrated hosts to bring over with me. I knew I wouldn't be able to attend Mass there, but wanted to be able to receive Communion.

My grandmother was also my Godmother, but our relationship wasn't very close. She had been away in Algeria and Tunisia for much of my childhood, and she also had a somewhat difficult personality. I found her very ill in bed, completely conscious, but communicating very little. She seemed like walled-in silence. My father, who had arrived a few days before me, was very concerned: 'What is she thinking, what's happening inside her?'

My aunt, who had been looking after her, was also concerned, not just by her physical condition, but by her silence. They would be both spending time at her bedside, but to no avail. They felt she had cut herself off.

I was on the sideline. I would call in briefly to see her, but there was little to no engagement, although her physical condition seemed to have stabilised. Death no longer seemed imminent.

The days passed. On the eve of my return flight home I realised I had one host left over in the pyx. It seemed a pity to bring it back to Dublin. That's when I had an inspiration.

I went into my grandmother's, sat beside her bed, and asked whether she would like me to pray with her. She indicated she would, so I said aloud a few short prayers and read one of the psalms. I could see she was listening. Then

I asked her whether she would like to receive Communion. She replied, 'Yes, but I wouldn't know how to receive'.

I told her it was very simple, that she had first received as a child and that I had a host and could give her Communion. So I gave her the last host in the pyx. It seemed as if it had been intended for her all along.

Afterwards, when I told my aunt and my father what I had done they were astonished. As we all knew, my grandmother had turned very much against religion and God, especially since the death of her husband, my grandfather. She intensely resented my aunt going to Mass.

So, of course, my father was incredulous: 'Did she know what she was doing, was she conscious?'

It was the last time I saw my grandmother alive. I felt it was very fitting that my parting 'gift' to her, who had been my Godmother at my baptism, was the Body of Christ.

The following morning I was back in Dublin. My grandmother had a few months' remission, which her doctor couldn't understand. He had never seen somebody in her condition last so long. My father told me she was much more at peace and had been more communicative with everyone. She had also asked to see a priest and received the Sacrament of the Sick. She finally died on Easter Monday, 12 April 1993. I returned for her funeral.

My grandmother's long drawn-out illness led to a surprising conversation with my father. He had stayed with her and would phone regularly to update me as the weeks passed by. Witnessing his mother's slow death must have re-awakened the memory of his wife's death, as he opened up to me in a way he had never before. But the question he asked me which obviously had been tormenting him took me aback: 'How do we know your mother is not still suffering?'

It was my turn to be astonished. In all the years my mother had been dead, such an idea had never crossed my mind, and I had had no inkling this had been on my father's mind for decades. How did he think she could still be suffering? He didn't elaborate, but I could only suppose he was thinking in terms of purgatory.

I responded: 'You announced to me her death by telling me "She is not suffering any longer". And that is the truth. The suffering is ours, because we are bereaved and miss her, but she, herself, is not suffering. The pain is ours, not hers.'

My father went on talking with me about his faith as he had never done before or since: 'How do I know I am not just talking to myself when I pray?' And he confided that the evening my mother had died he had read the Four Gospels, searching in vain for something. I could hear the reality of what a friend of his had told me: 'The day your mother died, the heavens shut down for your father.'

All I could do was listen to his still raw grief and share some of my own faith in that longest of phone calls. I subsequently wrote to him, but my father, after this exceptional openness, never broached the subject of my mother and death again.

I realised that while I had suffered terribly from my mother's loss, unlike my father I had been spared the added pain of believing she was still suffering. I never had any doubt she was free from all suffering. The child I was when she died believed she went straight to Heaven and was with God. If there was a Heaven and a God, she was there. If there wasn't, well the question of suffering was moot.

I wondered again what kind of God, what religion, my father had been fed in his early years which not only didn't comfort him but added such inner torment? *Dies irae*, the God of judgement?

൙ ൙ ൙

WHILE I WAS STRUGGLING TO GIVE expression to my sense of calling, meeting another woman who shared that same vocation prompted me to take the next step.

Delma Sheridan had studied in the Irish School of Ecumenics with me, but it was only now that she confided that she also felt called to the priesthood. She had experienced this call in childhood, had entered religious life which was the only path opened to her, but had left. Delma was a generation older than me and her long anguish at the blockage of her vocation resonated with my own suffering. After she had shared her story I was in tears and wondered: 'How many women are going to go to their graves with their vocations never acknowledged?'

Something had to be done. The idea came to me to launch a petition. One evening in February 1993, with Colm and Eamonn's help, the text of the petition was drafted on our kitchen table.

It read:

Petition for a New Partnership of Women and Men in the Roman Catholic Church.

'In Christ Jesus there is no longer male and female' (Galatians 3:28). We, the undersigned, believe that:

- Both men and women are equally created in the image of God

- Christ is equally present in both women and men
- The Spirit calls and gifts both women and men equally

We therefore petition that all ministries and offices in the Church be equally open to both women and men and all sexist structures and regulations be abolished.

After typing it up and printing it we started circulating it. The first signatures came from Colm's family. It was heartening that not only his parents signed, but also his grandmother, who was 98! She was a devout Catholic and had a brother who had been a Jesuit and two sisters who had been religious of the Sacred Heart but she could support a call for women to be ordained. She knew from her own personal experience that not all church rules are divine commands, far from it. When her husband had died the parish priest had told her and her son not to attend his funeral because it was in the Church of Ireland and against the rules, but she had ignored him and gone.

We then got friends and others to sign. The reception the petition got was very encouraging. It helped generate discussions. People in turn circulated it to others. It was laborious work, all pen and paper, as we were still decades before digital signing at the click of a button. But the handwritten signatures kept coming in, from all parts of the country. Several months later there was a good pile of them, and enquiries from several people: 'Is there a group we can join?'

We had to confess that there were only three of us behind the petition. But the seed had been planted about forming a group, as there seemed to be a hunger for one.

I initially resisted the idea. I thought it should really be an Irish woman, born and bred in Ireland, who should start this group for the ordination of women in Ireland. As a foreigner I didn't feel entitled to take the lead. However it slowly dawned on me that no Irish woman was forthcoming and that, by default, the role fell to me.

The name Brothers and Sisters in Christ and its acronym BASIC had come to me all at once, in a flash, while I was doing the ironing. I knew right away that's what the group was to be called. BASIC was launched on 6 November 1993, on the feast day of all the Irish Saints.

The cover of the BASIC leaflet featured a photo of a woman's hand (mine) and a man's hand (Eamonn's) holding a chalice. On my hand the wedding ring was clearly visible. This was to show that both women and men, married and celibate, can be called to the ministry.

On the back of the leaflet there was a prayer, 'Liberare', by a monk from Glenstal Abbey, Brother Basil. I had met him in Dublin and after hearing my story he had been moved to compose this prayer, which he dedicated to me. I had been struck by how it echoed both my grandmother's 'Memorare' and my youthful dream of the rebirth of freed women.

Liberare

> Enthused by the ancient promise,
> 'My mother, make your request
> For I will not refuse you'
> Mary, your sisters seek equity.

Confirmed at Cana, when your concern was eased.
In your many-sided mission
Remember your sisters' sorry state,
Bruised on the cross of disparity.

Mother of Beautiful Love,
'Like a vine we can cause loveliness to bud.'
Through the fullness of your grace
May the Holy Spirit erase the folly of favouritism.

Crying out Lord, Lord, open the door to us.
'Do not hide your Face
Forgetting our woe and oppression.'
Mary, enable your sisters to sing Libertae.[1]

Note: BASIC was incorporated into We Are Church Ireland in 2012.

ଊ ଊ ଊ

After my meeting with Bishop Murray it was time to take the message up the hierarchical ladder. I asked for a meeting with the Archbishop of Dublin, Desmond Connell, and I was given an appointment on 1 July 1993. I had read his piece against the ordination of women with its convoluted arguments. I had also corresponded with him about his 1991 Lenten Pastoral in which he mentioned the Subordination of Wives and had recommended I read Manfred Hauke's book *Women in the Priesthood*.

To my utter dismay, the book reminded me of some earlier pseudo-scientific propaganda, its absurd reasoning leading to the conclusion that 'the superiorities of men, to express things pointedly, lead to a position of authority, but

---
1 Libertae means freed women.

the superiorities of women, to a position of subordination.' I was looking forward, though with some trepidation, to telling him directly about my spiritual journey and sense of vocation.

But as I sat across from him at a highly polished table in a high-ceilinged room in Archbishop's House, I realised that wasn't going to happen. His purpose in agreeing to see me was to discharge his episcopal duty to show me the error of my ways, to set me right.

He had no interest in listening to anything I might share so it ended up a very one-sided conversation. I might as well have been one of his young philosophy students in UCD as he lectured me in a professorial tone on what I should believe. I only remember fragments.

His main argument was that, as he said plainly, 'Only a man can be on the cross, so only a man can be a priest and offer Mass.' For a split second I had a vision of all priests being nailed to crosses during Mass in our churches.

I didn't tell him about my painting of a woman on the cross and the accompanying poem about her being crucified, but I did object to his argument. Not on theological/sacramental grounds, which I had decided would be totally pointless, but on historical ones: 'Actually, there were women among the early Christians who were crucified in the early Roman persecutions. And when St Blandina was martyred in the arena in Lyon, attached to a pole and devoured by lions, it is reported that the spectators witnessed in her death a re-enactment of Christ's own passion and death. She was truly an Other Christ.'

He didn't say any more about men on crosses, but then tried to persuade me through an appeal to his episcopal authority. 'When I (and he emphasised the 'I') tell you that you do not have a calling to the priesthood, do you not hear God speaking to you?'

I was taken aback. It was of course a literal interpretation of 'Whoever listens to you, listens to me' (Luke 10:16). But the way he spoke, and especially the way he looked at me, reminded me of the scene in *The Jungle Book* when Kaa, the serpent, tries to hypnotise the boy Mowgli to devour him while saying, 'Trust me'.

'No, I hear you, my archbishop, speaking to me, not God,' I replied.

There wasn't much more. The archbishop wanted to spare me from following what he believed was a totally misguided and hopeless path to nowhere. But what he was saying found no resonance in me.

There had been no meeting of minds, hearts or spirits. No doubt he thought I was deluded and wrong-headed. I thought it was like trying to explain colours to a blind man. I felt he was on a totally different plane.

As we stood up and were shaking hands I spontaneously decided to reach out and I did what St Paul advise us to do: 'Greet each other with a holy kiss'. That was the only way I could think of bridging in some way the abyss of incomprehension between us. Being French I was of course well used to embracing and kissing all kinds of people, but it was the very first time I had kissed an archbishop, and so far the only one! I never was moved to repeat it.

The archbishop must have been surprised. He would have had more people planting a kiss on his ring than on his cheek, but he didn't seem offended at all by the familiarity. I was surprised, too, at my own daring.

Brothers and Sisters in Christ

ಆ   ಆ   ಆ

A FEW DAYS AFTER MY MEETING with Archbishop Connell, and still mulling over it, I met with Eamonn McCarthy. I asked him to drive to Tullow for a visit. I hadn't been back there since 1970, but now I felt the need to re-connect with my very first landing place in Ireland.

In particular, I wanted to go back to the church. We went into the empty building and prayed. On the way out I noticed some of the Catholic newspapers on display. I nearly laughed in amazement at what seemed to be a very quick answer to my prayer. The front page of one paper had in bold: 'Get Ready for Women Priests' says Schillebeeckx.

I read out loud the article to Eamonn: 'Church leaders must prepare Catholics to accept women priests by preaching very respectful, polite and serene homilies'. In his new book, *I Am a Happy Theologian*, the 79-year-old Dutch Dominican friar maintains that there are no theological obstacles to ordaining women and says the Church risks painful schisms if people are not prepared to accept the change. 'The Church of England's decision to ordain women priests was a great opening for ecumenism rather than an obstacle. Many Catholics are moving in that direction.'

He also supported optional celibacy for the priesthood. It was very affirming, but also challenging.

'I don't see Des Connell doing that kind of preaching,' I chuckled, 'or for that matter any other Irish bishops! It's going to be left to us to take a lead and do it.'

A Divine Calling

A month later I set out to meet the Bishop of Kildare and Leighlin which includes Tullow. Driving to Carlow I wondered what my younger self, aged 12 and 13, would have thought of my going to meet the local bishop to tell him I had a calling to priesthood. The path my life had taken seemed quite surreal, but also, strangely, very much true to my deepest self.

Bishop Larry Ryan received me very courteously. He did ask me why I wanted to be a priest, to which I replied it wasn't something I wanted. I felt called to it. This was the only honest answer I could give.

When the issue was raised that only men could be priests, I asked: 'What are women missing?' There was an awkward pause and I saw the bishop blushing. I then added, 'which of the gifts of the Spirit?' There was no answer.

It was a short meeting, and of course nothing really was achieved by it, but as I drove home to Dublin I had a sense it had been important for me, for the young girl who had arrived in Tullow in 1969 and who still lived in me.

I met Bishop Ryan once again, a few years later, at a gathering in Clonliffe, where he was going to talk about St Thérèse. Before his talk I made a statement about St Thérèse wanting to be a priest. He later joked I had 'stolen his thunder', but he did conceded that he wouldn't have mentioned this particular fact!

ଓ ଓ ଓ

I WAS AT HOME ONE EVENING WATCHING a television programme on the Knock Shrine when I experienced a strong desire to go there as a family. I had never been there before. When Colm came home from his weekly Saint Vincent de

Paul visitation I told him of that desire. 'That's funny,' he replied, 'because Jimmy has just asked me to drive him to Knock.' Jimmy was a wheelchair user Colm regularly visited.

'Great!' I said, 'when are we going?'

'Not for a while, Jimmy mentioned he wanted to go in the autumn.'

The months passed and we finally set out at the end of November with our two young sons and collected Jimmy in Dublin City centre before taking the road west. We arrived in Knock under a very grey sky. It was deserted, damp, cold and windy and very bleak looking indeed. This was before the renovation of the basilica and landscaping of the surroundings.

We managed to find somewhere to eat and walked to the old church for Mass in the afternoon.

The boys took turns to push Jimmy in his wheelchair. Jimmy had nicknamed the oldest 'uphill' and the youngest 'downhill' as they shared the effort!

There were very few people inside the little old church. We sat down and Jimmy promptly fell fast asleep. The priest on the altar mentioned in his homily that while he was Irish he had ministered many years in France. As he proceeded with the rest of the liturgy, the thought suddenly popped into my head to ask him to bless my vocation. I had no reason to think the priest was in favour of women priests and my rational mind argued it was a preposterous idea.

Mass ended. Jimmy woke up and said, 'I must get the blessing of the sick!' So we all trooped into the sacristy. The priest was taking off his vestments as I greeted the sister at the door who immediately picked up on my accent.

'Father, there is a French woman,' she called out.

The priest quickly came over and said, 'I must give you a blessing'. He then prayed over me in Latin. I marvelled how it all happened, I hadn't even had to make my request.

Jimmy protested, 'I am the sick person, I am the one to get a blessing.' And yes, he did get his blessing too.

When we finally arrived home after the long drive home I told Colm what had happened. I had been called to Knock to have my vocation blessed, although I certainly didn't know it beforehand! From that time on Knock has been a very special place for me.

That day, 27 November, was the feast day of the 'miraculous medal' commemorating Mary's apparition to St Catherine Labouré in Rue du Bac. I had often prayed in the chapel when in Paris.

5.

A Woman of Sorrow

One of the thoughts which preoccupied me was whether the pope had ever met with women who had a sense of vocation to the ordained ministries. I believed it was very important that as head of the Church (under Christ) he should know what was happening in the lives of women. After all, he should at least be informed properly. I came to believe that I had to try to do something about it.

I didn't know where to start, having absolutely no connections in the higher rungs of the Church hierarchy, but I got an idea when I read an article in *The Tablet* about an order of nuns coming to the diocese of Cloyne at the invitation of the bishop, John Magee. Bishop Magee had been Private Secretary to Pope Paul VI, Pope John Paul I and Pope John Paul II before coming back to Ireland. I wrote to him asking for a meeting, mentioning the articles about the nuns and my sense of vocation, but nothing more. I thought if I mentioned the priesthood I would get a refusal. He replied at once offering me a meeting in early December on his return from travelling.

When I wrote back to accept I felt I should tell the truth and specify it was about a vocation to the priesthood. I didn't want him to feel I had tricked him. He didn't write back to cancel so I headed off to Cobh on 10 December 1993.

It was a long journey back then, with no motorway, and my appointment was mid-morning so I travelled the evening before and stayed in a B&B. As I lay in bed away from my family I recall wondering what on earth had possessed me to make that trip. As I tossed and turned I was tempted to cancel the meeting and go back to Dublin at first light.

In the morning I plucked up my courage and went to the cathedral for Mass. It was Advent and there was a tree of Jesse in the sanctuary. I was further encouraged when the priest mentioned that today the name of Ruth was to be added on the tree, Ruth the foreigner, like me.

Then I was in the bishop's office. John Magee received me very courteously. He didn't seem shocked I had that sense of vocation, but he asked me why I wanted to be a priest. 'Is it because of the status? Is it to say Mass? To preach? Or is it for another reason?'

I was astonished when he mentioned status which had never crossed my mind. Where I came from, there wasn't much status attached to being a priest. It was a religious vocation, that's all. And of course the ones who had inspired me were the worker priests. Later I understood how his question made sense in Ireland, where the clergy still had a certain standing.

Anyway I said, no, status didn't enter into it, and really it was more that I felt called to it rather than deciding to pursue it. John Magee listened attentively. He then offered me a piece of encouragement.

'I met with Mother Teresa and she told me she had had great difficulties in getting her new order recognised by Rome. The nuncio had once said disparagingly that this woman has difficulties lighting candles, how could she start an order? But she persevered, so don't get discouraged.'

I then asked him whether the pope had ever met with women like me and he replied, 'No, not to my knowledge, certainly not while I was still there'. The meeting ended with me giving him one of the freshly printed BASIC brochures.

I was quite elated when I left him. It was a crisp and bright winter day as I drove back to Dublin, pondering our exchange. We exchanged Christmas cards for several years.

I did ask him in a letter whether he could help arrange for me to meet Pope John Paul II. What I didn't know at the time was that John Magee had left Rome under a cloud so he couldn't be of much help to me. Later, of course, there would be the Cloyne Report and Bishop Magee would have to resign. But all that was still in the future. It remains that I felt heard, respected and even encouraged at a time when it made a difference,

There is one last amusing anecdote: A fireball identified as a meteorite had plunged into Cobh Harbour the evening I arrived there. A narrow miss!

೮ ೮ ೮

My strong belief that Catholic Church leaders should know that there were women with a sense of vocation naturally led me to contact Cardinal Cahal Daly. Cardinal Daly was Archbishop of Armagh and therefore Primate of all Ireland, the highest rung on the clerical hierarchy in Ireland.

One of his predecessors in Armagh, Cardinal Tomás O'Fiaich, had an open attitude to women's ordination. He was quoted in *The Curia is the Pope* by John O'Loughlin Kennedy as saying:

> There is no reason in Dogmatic Theology why women should not be priests. There is no reason in Biblical Studies why women should not be priests, but they won't be priests, because the body of men required to make that decision is incapable of making that decision.

However, I was soon to discover that Cardinal Daly was a resolute opponent. I first wrote to him in June 1993 requesting a meeting. His reply was that it would be a waste of time, like a 'dialogue of the deaf – even if it might seem to you the deafness were only on my side!' I insisted that 'we both believe in a God who can cure deafness', and therefore we should meet.

I must have convinced him because I got a letter agreeing to a meeting, but since he was busy it wouldn't be until after the summer. I patiently waited until September and rang his office in Armagh, explaining why I was telephoning. The priest secretary replied he would pass on my message to the cardinal. I waited for a letter or phone call with a date for our meeting, but nothing came. I phoned again a few weeks later, but I got the same answer.

Christmas and the New Year passed by with still complete silence from Armagh. I was wondering whether I should phone yet again, which seemed ineffective, or just give up altogether on the idea of meeting with the cardinal. But hadn't he agreed to meet me, in writing? I reasoned that if he had changed his mind, he should at least tell me.

It was now early February 1994. With Valentine's day approaching I suddenly had an inspiration. Instead of phoning I would send a card as a reminder! I spent a long time looking for a suitable Valentine's card. After all, none were designed for a cardinal for the purpose I had in mind!

I eventually found one that was fairly bland and wrote inside, 'You have promised me a meeting, what about a DATE?' I posted my card marked Personal and waited. On February 17 a letter arrived from the cardinal: 'Thank you for your card. You are very patient. Can you come on Saturday, March 5, at 11.00 am?

I phoned the secretary to confirm I would be there. I wondered whether he had seen my Valentine's card. Was it my imagination or was I hearing some amusement in his voice? In any case, I now had a date with the cardinal thanks to the intercession of St Valentine.

Ten days later Colm and I went into Dublin city centre to organise our first public day of prayer for the ordination of women on March 25. We ended up in Easons on O'Connell Street, looking for paper to print posters for the vigil. I looked up from the shelves and saw Cardinal Daly, here in Dublin, on his own! I couldn't believe it. I went over and introduced myself. He must have been startled too.

'We have a date,' I said.

'Yes, indeed, we have. Do you know your way to Armagh?'

'I will follow the star.'

Colm and I both thought it was very funny, especially since the cardinal didn't know yet about this forthcoming public prayer event for women's ordination.

I was now counting the days to my meeting with Cardinal Daly. The Sunday evening before, I had gone to bed early with the Sunday papers when the phone rang. 'Ms Vatinel? This is Cardinal Daly.' My heart sank, I thought he was going to cancel our meeting, but no. 'Could you please come an hour earlier on Saturday morning? I have to meet some people afterwards. It was very nice meeting you in Easons.'

I was relieved: 'Of course, no problem at all, I'll be there.'

The long awaited day for my meeting with Cardinal Daly finally arrived. Eamonn McCarthy had agreed to drive me there, for companionship and support, which meant I could prepare myself for the meeting and not be stressed by driving in unfamiliar territory.

We crossed the border and arrived in Armagh in very good time. We went into the cathedral up on a hill to pray. I remember being drawn to the stained glass window of St Patrick baptising young women, St Eithne and St Fidelma. And then it was time for me to ring the bell of the cardinal's residence, Ara Caeli. Eamonn chose to wait in the car.

I was ushered into a waiting room. As I sat down I saw in front of me the cardinal's red hat beside a small suitcase. There was also a mirror in the room, so the temptation was very strong to put on the hat and look at myself in the mirror. But on this occasion I resisted. I reckoned that as soon as I put on the red hat the door would open and that wouldn't be a good start to the meeting.

So I waited patiently until I was brought to meet the cardinal. I remember feeling the depth of the carpet under my feet walking there. Of my actual conversation with the cardinal I remember only some fragments.

What I didn't know at the time was that he was an ardent opponent of women's ordination and had been trying to dissuade the Anglicans from going ahead with it. I must have pointed out that the Church had moved on from considering women as inferior and wives as subordinates, because he vehemently denied it. 'The Church *never* taught the subordination of wives!' He wasn't looking at me as he said it, but out the window, which means he didn't see the sceptical look on my face.

'That's just a lie,' I thought to myself but didn't voice it. However he must have felt unsure of his own ground as he proceeded to tell me that in his parents' marriage it was his mother who was the strong one, and she was the one who made the decisions. This of course was a complete red herring.

And on and on it went; there certainly was no meeting of minds. The cardinal was trying to convince me with all his might that I was wrong, while I grew increasingly silent. It was like a boxing match but I had no gloves on. I was mortified when I started crying.

There was a small pause as a woman entered: 'Will your Eminence have coffee?'

As coffee was being served I had time to ponder this 'Your Eminence' title and the power attached to it. Not for the first time I wondered what it did to the men who had it, and how far from the simplicity of the Gospel we had travelled. Here was power speaking to me.

The meeting was coming to an end when the cardinal dropped a bombshell of a question: 'What would you do if the pope was to make an infallible declaration against the ordination of women?'

I was stunned at the thought. That possibility had never entered my head. As far as I was concerned the discussion on women's ordination was only getting started in earnest. So why was he suggesting something like that, the papal heavy gun of an infallible declaration? It didn't make any sense to me. What could I say? All I could reply was, 'God has never abandoned me in the past and will not in the future'.

Cardinal Daly looked at me pensively: 'I admire your faith'. What did he really think? Of course he knew what was being prepared in Rome, while I was totally ignorant of what was coming my way. After that, there was nothing left to say. I decided I would ask for a blessing, which I got, and he asked me to pray for him. After an hour and a half of this 'dialogue of the deaf' I left very distraught. It had been a difficult, painful meeting.

We went to have some lunch but I had no appetite. Because it was still at the height of the Troubles there were armed soldiers at every street corner. The threat of violence was in the air. There was no solace in Armagh for my aching heart. I couldn't wait to leave.

It was just as well Eamonn was driving as I couldn't stop weeping all the way back. There had been no dialogue; it was like meeting a stone wall. I felt bruised all over, drained, defeated, crushed. And this hinting at an 'infallible papal declaration' was now a menacing dark cloud over me, darker than the grey sky that was over us.

'God has never abandoned me and will not in the future.' My belief would soon be tested beyond my imagining, but not before making my television debut in France.

ಬ ಬ ಬ

EARLY IN 1994 I RECEIVED A PHONE call asking me if I would participate in a French television programme to speak about my vocation to be a Catholic priest. Although French, I had been living in Ireland for over twenty years, so I replied I would only do so if they really couldn't find somebody in France. They told me nobody else was willing to go public and I was the only one they could find.

So I flew from Dublin to Paris to appear on live television. I had spoken on radio but never on television, so this was another step. It amused me that my debut on television should be in my home country. I had a sense of God opening doors to me in a way I could never have dreamt of, so this was just the latest adventure on a very unusual journey.

On Friday, 11 March (the anniversary of my poem 'A Woman of Sorrow'), I left my father's house in Versailles to take the suburban train to the television studio in Paris. On my way I stopped off at the Church of St Joan of Arc and said a prayer asking to be guided in my television contribution. I was calm and collected, and aware of God's supporting presence.

But as the train pulled out of the station, it all changed rapidly and inexplicably. It was as if I was suddenly plunged in darkness and an inner voice filled me with dread: 'Not only are you deceiving yourself that you are called to be a priest, but you are going to go and deceive all these people!' I was now in a pit of despair. There was absolutely no way I could continue and appear in public, if my vocation was a lie.

As I was sitting with my private agony a busker appeared in the carriage and started singing. After a few verses he stopped and declared to the passengers:

'I am going to tell you the story of Mary of Nazareth. At the foot of the Cross she said to God, "I offer Him back to you, my flesh and blood".' That's all he said.

As I heard these unexpected words, my inner darkness lifted, the oppressive voice was silenced and replaced by a deep peace. The storm was stilled miraculously and I was saved from drowning. The busker then went to exit the carriage. I gave him a handsome tip; his words were well worth it!

The television discussion went very smoothly.

There was another miracle linked to this event. I hadn't told anybody in France besides my father that I would be on television to reveal to the nation that I had a calling to the priesthood. But later I discovered that my brother was in hospital following a minor accident and watching afternoon TV, and also that my best friend Pascaline happened to turn on that channel at that time. Imagine their surprise to see me on screen with that revelation: A real 'coming out'! I couldn't have organised it better than Providence did.

My father, of course, had watched the discussion, but again he didn't say very much except to suggest I shouldn't have laughed, as I had at some point in the interview. 'Why not? Some things are truly ridiculous.' But he couldn't see the humour in it as I did.

When I had told him over the phone I had sent a Valentine's card to Cardinal Daly as a last ditch attempt at getting a meeting, he hadn't been impressed: 'These people in the hierarchy are very important, you cannot treat them in such a cavalier fashion, you'll get nowhere.' By then I had figured out that 'these people' had an inflated sense of their own importance and took themselves far too seriously. I just couldn't go along with it. My father was wrong – I got the meeting in Armagh – but he was right too as I got nowhere with the hierarchy!

It was also around that time when I read in my father's daily newspaper, *The Figaro*, a column by the famous writer André Frossard on the subject of women priests. In it he completely dismissed the idea, with specious arguments such as Jesus not choosing women as apostles because he wanted to spare them the violent deaths that the men would meet.

I was incensed at what I considered to be nonsense. I wrote a reply to the writer in which I cited all the women martyrs, and that St Paul himself had confessed having persecuted 'both men and women' before his conversion.

My father's reaction took me by surprise: 'You can't challenge him. He is a very powerful man.' I could see he was visibly afraid, afraid for me. André Frossard, author of *God Exists, I Have Met Him*, was a member of the French Academy and a close and influential friend of Pope John Paul II.

'So what?' I replied. 'What he writes is not true at all.'

'He is very well connected, you don't know what he will do.'

To my father's dismay I posted the letter. Needless to say, I never heard a word back. But I had seen my father's fear: the Catholic Church is a powerful institution so one shouldn't take it on. He only wanted to protect me. I think through the next decades until his death in 2016 these things remained with him: An awareness of the suffering involved, and a fear for me as I increasingly exposed myself to powerful forces in the Church.

ಐ ಐ ಐ

I WAS BACK IN DUBLIN IN TIME TO celebrate the first World Day of Prayer for Women's Ordination in the Catholic Church.

A Divine Calling

We had chosen 25 March, the Feast of the Annunciation. It was gratifying to hear that a group in Australia, Women of the New Covenant, had also picked that date, completely independently. We were seventy-two souls (a good Biblical number) gathered on a chilly spring evening in O'Connell Street. We held our prayer vigil outside the GPO – symbolically, another Easter Rising – as we prayed and sang under a banner proclaiming:

**Imagine Women Priests in the Catholic Church
by the Year 2000**

We lit a tall candle in the darkness: There was hope and joy as passerbys on foot and passengers from buses came across this unusual scene. We have had many celebrations on 25 March since, but that first one remains vivid in my mind. Announcing boldly to the world God was doing a new thing in the Church. Our Annunciation. Imagine!

ಬಿ ಬಿ ಬಿ

IN MAY 1992 I WAS GIVEN MY first opportunity to take part in a formal Church consultation process. The Council of Priests in the Archdiocese of Dublin had decided they wanted 'to listen to the pain of women in the Church'. For that purpose they set up a sub-committee of four priests who were to co-opt four women. Eamonn McCarthy was one of the priests and he asked me. It was a new experience and I entered into it with a sense of commitment. But the writing was already on the wall. Archbishop Connell apparently had told the priests on the sub-committee not to discuss the ordination of women.

Our sub-committee of four women and four priests met regularly for over a year and a half. It quickly emerged that there was pressure to censor ourselves. One priest in particular was adamant that some topics couldn't, and shouldn't, be mentioned. Women's ordination in particular was anathema to him. It wasn't that he was against it, but he was fearful of the archbishop's reaction.

'What is the worst that can happen?' I asked.

'He'll get angry and storm out of the room,' he replied.

'Well, if he chooses to respond like that, so be it.'

I argued we had been tasked with speaking about women's pain in the Church, and we would fail if we only spoke about what was acceptable to the archbishop. He might as well just listen to himself was my view. I was determined I would not be silenced: I would speak my pain.

I couldn't believe how fearful that senior priest was as I had known him as an outspoken lecturer in Milltown. It was an eye opener. In later years I would meet many more priests like him, afraid of confronting the powers that be with an honest opinion.

On 23 February 1994 we gathered in a large room in Clonliffe College to hand over our report and make a verbal presentation to the assembled Council of Priests, with the archbishop and auxiliary bishops. Our colleague on the subcommittee chose to sit well apart from us, in a safe place among the other clerics.

We four women took turns in sharing our experiences in the Church, especially the painful aspects, and gave our recommendations, as was our brief. The issue of altar girls, still officially forbidden, was one of them. When my turn finally came I spoke of my sense of calling to the presbyteral ministry. It took all the courage I could muster to share it with all these clerics present. I was acutely aware of the intense resistance to what I was saying and the level of discomfort in the room. I finished by reading 'A Woman of Sorrow', which I had written the previous year when Eamonn had urged me to write about my life, faith and vocation. All my attempts had failed because of the immense pain for which I struggled to find words. In the end all that came out was 'A Woman of Sorrow', giving words to that Crucified Woman I had painted the year before.

A Woman of Sorrow

> An object of curiosity or rejection,
> she hangs,
> bloodied and bruised,
> stripped of her dignity,
> crucified on the cross
> of her calling.
> Above her head it is written:
> 'Woman priest'
> The blind crowd jeers and mocks,
> spitting God, Scripture and Tradition
> to her face
> 'God chooses only men'.
> 'You're a neurotic, get your head examined'.
> 'You lack humility, you want power'.
> If only she would recant,
> confess her deluded arrogance.
> Many turn away,
> a few stand by her.

A Woman of Sorrow

> For eighteen years now
> she has been bound
> her womanhood derided
> her youthful life ebbing away
> in an endless agony.
> Only silence answers her screaming broken heart
> Church – forsaken
> God – forsaken.
>
> Through her tears
> she sees Him at her side
> the loving, gentle Christ
> who called her, still a girl
> to serve Him.
> Bloodied and bruised,
> crucified on the cross of His calling,
> and yet smiling:
> 'Woman, they did not receive Me,
> and so they do not receive you,
> for they do not love enough'.

The archbishop didn't storm out of the room. There was just an awkward silence, and then it was over. We were formally thanked and given lunch. After months of hard work and intense preparation, that was it. There was no further contact.

A few months later I received a phone call from a journalist with *The Tablet*, Margaret Hebblethwaite, in London. Margaret knew of my advocacy for women's ordination and expressed her puzzlement at seeing my name attached to a report expressly ruling it out. It was my turn to be puzzled.

'What report?'

'It's the Report of the Dublin Council of Priests,' explained Margaret.

The Report of the Dublin Council of Priests on Women in the Church had been sent out far and wide with accompanying press releases, and we, the female members of the sub-committee, had never seen it. Our names, however, were prominently included.

Margaret Hebblethwaite couldn't believe it, and I couldn't believe it either. As she read out the contents of the report, I felt physically sick at what, for me, was a betrayal. No wonder Margaret had queried why my name was included. The report, approved by the archbishop, stated: 'The fact that the priesthood was given only to men did not prevent women from taking their full part in the life of the Church.'

I was stunned and furious. The next day an extract from the report appeared in the *Irish Catholic* newspaper, with my name and that of the other women.

I wrote to the priest chairing the Council of Priests, with copies to the auxiliary bishops, to express how I felt about the report, both its content and the manner of its release. The priest replied that this was a report of the Council of Priests, of which I was not a member. I had only been a member of the subcommittee, and so had no grounds to complain.

It was clear that the fact my name and those of the other women appeared with the report didn't matter. This was obviously just window dressing: after all, we had been consulted! And why did I think I was entitled to the basic courtesy of a copy of the report?

I felt used and manipulated. I wrote back that if that was the way they treated lay people, they wouldn't get too many in the future. It was a painful lesson that I would not forget.

ஐ ஐ ஐ

GOING TO MASS ON SUNDAYS HAD now become an ordeal. It didn't matter where or in which Church , whether in Dublin or in France while on holidays, or who the priest was. It was not about anything specific. It was just being present at Mass which caused me such inner suffering that tears would start rolling down my cheeks. I would weep silently throughout the liturgy. It was as if there was a crushing of my spirit.

Colm would kneel, sit or stand beside me, aware of my pain and helpless at relieving it. After witnessing it for nearly a year, he eventually raised the question: 'If it is causing you such pain every time, should you continue going to Mass?' It was a valid question for which I had as yet no answer.

The Eucharist was such a vital part of me, of my life, and yet it was also causing me intense distress. The passage of time wasn't alleviating it; every Sunday I would come back from Mass drained, with eyes red and burning, broken hearted. Why put myself through this hardship week after week? Should I stop going? But then what?

Around that time I came across an article by Ronald Rolheiser, OMI, 'Alive with Prophetic Pain', which put words on what I was experiencing and told me I wasn't alone:

> In the Eucharist, among other things, the passion and death of Christ are being re-enacted. Obviously,

those who are suffering the most and are doing some dying, are the Christ figures. That is why it is so important those who feel like these women, those who fill with pain and tears at the Eucharist, remain in the Church and remain at the Eucharist. Without prophetic tears, we grow ever more deaf. And prophets die somewhere between altar and sanctuary. But their groan is a word, a voice that cannot be killed.

Yes, stay at the Eucharist, but this was a way of staying which wasn't what Rolheiser had in mind, or me either!

As for people hearing the pain, I remember the retired parish priest of Booterstown, Jerome Curtin, asking me incredulously, 'Surely the pain isn't that bad?' Yes it is, I replied, but under no illusion that it would make any difference. I knew he expressed a widely held view. To really hear the pain would mean not dismissing it as hysterical but seeing it as prophetic. It would mean acknowledging that something was amiss and needed to be rectified.

ଓ଼ ଓ଼ ଓ଼

OUR VOICES MAY HAVE BEEN 'A VOICE that cannot be killed' and yet this is exactly what the Church authorities attempted to do with Pope John Paul II's Apostolic Letter *Ordinatio Sacerdatolis* (On Reserving Priestly Ordination to Men Alone).

Signed on Pentecost Sunday, it was released on 30 May 1994, on the feast day of St Joan of Arc. With the news, that bright sunny day turned suddenly cold and dark. Despite what Cardinal Daly had hinted at during our meeting, I hadn't expected this move. It took me, and almost everybody else, completely by surprise.

I read it with disbelief. It was like reading a spiritual death sentence:

> Wherefore, in order that all doubt may be removed regarding a matter which pertains to the Church's divine constitution itself.... I declare that the Church has no authority whatsoever to confer priestly ordination on women and that this judgment is to be definitely held by all the Church's faithful.

The debate was to be forcibly closed.

One of the sources of this doubt to be removed, at all cost, was the testimony of women like me. We would have to be silenced, disbelieved, ignored, made invisible, removed.

I experienced *Ordinatio Sacerdatolis* as an act of extreme violence. While couched in spiritual language and invoking Christ, it had none of the liberating, uplifting power of the Gospel. Instead, it had the hallmarks of a dominant hierarchical patriarchal system panicking as its power is slipping away. Batten down the hatches. Lift up the drawbridge. Close and barricade the door.

A decade later, retired Bishop Geoffrey Robinson would make public some of the manipulation, deception and bullying behind *Ordinatio Sacerdatolis*. In early 1994, the Presidents of the Episcopal Conferences of the world were summoned to Rome. Cardinal Daly would have gone, hence his foreknowledge. They were presented with *Ordinatio Sacerdatolis*, ready for publication. It included an obviously untrue statement to the effect that it had been prepared 'having heard the views of the bishops'. The Presidents were asked to approve it on behalf of their bishops. They refused on the very reasonable ground that they would have to consult the bishops first, otherwise it would be a lie.

But consulting the bishops would have only resulted in more 'doubt' being aired rather than removed, and would have fuelled the debate rather than closing it. So the Apostolic Letter was published with no bishop having been consulted.

There was no reason even to pretend any woman had been consulted: What would we know about what God is doing in our lives? No need to listen to us when the pope and the Curia have a direct line to the Almighty.

The violence at the core of *Ordinatio Sacerdatolis* enabled the latent misogyny in the Church to become even more open and virulent: The pope has spoken. The door is closed. The debate is over. For *ever*. The pope has said 'No'. What part of 'No' do you not understand? It's over. Now go away.

The intention was to kill the hope that our vocation would be someday fulfilled, that rejection would be replaced by a welcome, disbelief by recognition. Abandon ye all hope, accept that the Church's position cannot and will not change.

'God has never abandoned me in the past and God will not in the future.' I could only cling to these words that I had uttered to Cardinal Daly only three months ago. Hang on to hope.

While it all looked very bleak I decided I had to take a step, even a small one, to convey that hope. On the feast day of the Sacred Heart, I went to the Divine Master Liturgical Centre nearby and commissioned a stole. I asked for it to be embroidered with the Sacred Heart and Mary's Heart. The sister who took the order, presuming it was a gift, asked me if it was urgent. When was the ordination? Could I wait until after the summer? I replied I certainly could. I collected it in the autumn on the feast day of Our Lady of Sorrows. Over the years I would be gifted many more stoles, including one from Jerusalem by a priest. You cannot kill hope, though Rome did try with all its might.

Not surprisingly, my poem 'A Woman of Sorrow' was one of the first casualties of *Ordinatio Sacerdatolis*. I had sent it to the Redemptorist magazine *Reality* and it had been accepted for publication later in 1994. The editor regretfully informed me that the editorial board had decided it was no longer possible. Censorship had started. The crucified Woman of Sorrow had no place in this new Church.

ഔ ഔ ഔ

WHILE MY REQUESTS FOR A PRIVATE audience with the pope remained unanswered, there was still the possibility of attending a public one. Not what I wanted of course, but I reckoned I may at least have an opportunity to hand over a letter directly to the pope. Before *Ordinatio Sacerdatolis* had been published we already had planned a family holiday in Italy. It would be my first time back in Rome and to my beloved Assisi since 1975.

On 13 July we set out from the Irish College where we were staying to attend the weekly general audience. The theme chosen was auspicious, or rather ironic: 'The role of women in the Church'! Pope John Paul II was on a large platform – surrounded exclusively by men, clerics and Swiss guards – and spoke at length about us, women, who made up more than half of the packed hall. I don't remember what the pope actually said. Did it even matter? The

A Divine Calling

optics screamed it all very loudly: the role of women is to listen to men who speak for them, and down to them. Then came the time for a Scripture reading. It was John's Gospel where Mary of Magdala is commissioned by the Risen Christ to 'go and tell', making her the apostle to the apostles. I couldn't believe my ears: the Gospel was read in several languages, each time by a different cleric. Not one woman's voice was heard!

I thought how Mary of Magdala wouldn't be impressed, nor would the Risen Christ who entrusted her with the Good News. It was totally absurd. The crowd, like any fan club, applauded and took photos. I remained silent, taking in what I had just witnessed.

I had asked our ten-year-old son Jonathan to try to deliver my letter to the pope, as I knew I wouldn't be let near him. I watched him valiantly make several attempts, but each time was rebuffed by the heavy security. Defeated, he handed me back the letter I had carefully crafted. I comforted him, but in truth I also needed comforting. I felt spiritually bruised. I was glad our next stop was Assisi.

ဢ ဢ ဢ

Rome may have spoken, but it did not stop the discussion completely. I was contacted by RTÉ who asked me to be filmed as part of a TV programme on women priests for their *Would You Believe?* series, and I readily agreed.

Gemma McCrohan was the interviewer. The filming was a new experience but I got on well with the RTÉ team who were respectful and gave me an opportunity to share my spiritual journey and sense of calling. They did ask me whether they could film me praying in church, but I refused. If I knew I was being filmed I would not be able to pray, and I didn't want to pretend to pray for the camera. They respected my decision.

When the programme was shown on 8 February 1995, I was pleased with the result. In it another woman, a member of the Church of Ireland, also married with a family, was interviewed and described how the call came to her one day in church. The difference between how that call was heard and received in her church compared to mine was made very plain. While she was told, 'Why not?' and entered a training process where the call could lead to ordination, the response to mine was a resounding '*No*'. In the programme Father Brendan Leahy (now Bishop of Limerick) was interviewed to give the reasons why the Catholic Church didn't ordain women. No, it wasn't discrimination against women, he assured the interviewer, it's just women aren't men and only men can be priests.

In the programme I also mentioned that we had collected 10,000 signatures to the BASIC petition, and that I had written to Cardinal Daly, on behalf of the group, asking him to receive them. That was many months earlier and there had been no response from the cardinal, well, not until that request had been made public in the *Would You Believe?* programme. Two days later I received a reply from Cardinal Daly informing me that he wouldn't receive the petition because it 'would be an act of disobedience to the pope in a grave matter'.

I decided that his reaction should be made public, as the issue of the petition had been aired on *Would You Believe?* I sent a letter to *The Irish Times*. While it had taken Cardinal Daly several months and a TV programme to reply, negatively, to my request to receive the petition, now it took him just two days to send me an angry response:

> I have to say that the knowledge that extracts from a personal correspondence between me and yourself can find its way into public print in a newspaper does create certain problems for me, and must impose a certain restraint on what I might write in any further correspondence with you. I regret this and indeed confess that I am very disappointed by it.

As I read his letter I felt guilty for a moment, but then realised how manipulative it really was. I hadn't written about a private matter. I had written to him on BASIC notepaper in my capacity as its spokesperson. Plus, 10,000 Irish people had signed that petition and deserved to know why he, an official Church representative, wouldn't receive it. He was entitled to say 'no' which had to be respected, but I also was entitled to communicate his refusal to the people who had signed. I wrote to him making these points. Needless to say, I never got an acknowledgment.

But I had learned a lot about manipulation and abuse of power in the Church. Years later, when I heard about how victims of sexual violence by clerics had been treated by Church leaders, I had no difficulty believing the dreadful treatment they received.

๛ ๛ ๛

IF *ORDINATIO SACERDATOLIS* HAD INTENDED to put an end to any talk of women's ordination, it had failed. Instead, it spurred us on to give greater voice to the issue. We would not be cowed into silence. We would be heard! A seminar was organised by BASIC on the feast of the Annunciation, 25 March 1995. Would anybody come, now that the pope had spoken?

The bookings came thick and fast from all corners of Ireland, and the large hall was packed with a lively crowd. The candle which had been lit a year earlier outside the GPO was lit again and the words of the Taizé chant filled the room:

> In the Lord, I'll be ever thankful,
> In the Lord I will rejoice!
> Look to God, do not be afraid,
> Lift up your voices,
> The Lord is near.

Mary McAleese was the first to speak. I can still hear her opening words ringing in my ears: 'They say the debate is closed. I think they had better turn up their hearing aids.' It was an electrifying speech.

When my turn came to speak, as the last of three Catholic women with a vocation to the priesthood, I found that I could not stand: My legs just would not carry me. I had to sit down. But my voice did not fail me. I hadn't written down a speech, but I spoke from my heart about my faith and calling.

Some had warned me not to mention that I had had a breakdown while in college, but I felt it was an important part of my story. I spoke plainly about the pain I experienced: 'I have not been sexually abused but I have been profoundly spiritually abused by my own Church, the Church whom I deeply love'. I read out 'A Woman of Sorrow' and showed to the audience my painting of the Woman on the

Cross. I concluded with the powerfully moving witness of Sister Irene McCormack, who had presided the Eucharist in the Andes in Peru when there were no priests left. She was not crucified, but shot dead by the Shining Path.

After I finished, people stood up and applauded. I was humbled and comforted: I had been heard. Inside I felt as if I had emptied myself of what I had carried for so long. The last speaker was Professor Enda McDonagh from Maynooth who declared: 'The admission of women to all forms of ministry in the Roman Catholic Church is a truth that cannot finally be denied – it is something that will come.'

That night RTÉ News showed some of Mary McAleese's speech and also Church of Ireland priest Reverend Margaret Gilbert officiating at the wedding of her daughter earlier that day.

The contributions, including the discussions, were recorded and later published in a book. In early November all of the speakers gathered at Áras an Uachtaráin to present a copy of the book to President Mary Robinson. It was a very proud moment. As we posed for a group photo in the autumn sunshine none of us guessed that the next president of Ireland was in our midst: two years later Mary McAleese would succeed Mary Robinson.

ಬಾ   ಬಾ   ಬಾ

IN THE AFTERNOON OF 23 NOVEMBER 1995 I received a phone call from Peter Steinfels from *The New York Times*. Peter, who wrote on religious affairs, had previously reported on BASIC. 'What is your response to the latest Vatican statement on the ordination of women?'

'What statement?'

A Woman of Sorrow

'What, you don't know? Haven't you heard?' he sounded incredulous.

'No. What is it?'

'The Congregation for the Doctrine of the Faith (CDF) has declared that the teaching in *Ordinatio Sacerdatolis* on the non-ordination of women belongs to the Deposit of Faith.' This was contained in a document *Responsum Ad Dubium* signed on 28 October 1995, but which was only just released.

My heart sank. I took a deep breath. This was serious: another turn of the key in the lock of the closed door to women priests. More repression.

Peter went on: 'Has it not been reported in Ireland? It has been everywhere else, it's big news.'

I thought for a few seconds. 'Well, I think I know why we haven't heard: We are voting tomorrow in a referendum to remove the ban on divorce.'

After I put down the phone, I made my way to the Catholic Press Office which was nearby in Booterstown. In response to my enquiry they confirmed my hunch: Yes, they had the Vatican statement however somebody higher up had decided to embargo its release for a few days, until after the divorce referendum vote. But since I knew of the statement, well, yes I could have a copy.

I was determined Irish Catholics wouldn't be kept in the dark about what the rest of the world knew. That embargo was thoroughly manipulative on the part of the Irish bishops. I went to the RTÉ Television News desk with the statement. The CDF declaration made the main evening news, together with my response. The media carried it the following morning, the day of the vote, with a big article in

The Irish Times. The Referendum narrowly passed by 9,000 votes.

The 1995 *Responsum Ad Dubium* was explosive because for the first time it introduced the word infallible in relation to the non-ordination of women.

> The teaching requires definitive assent, since, founded on the written word of God, and from the beginning constantly preserved and applied in the tradition of the Church, it has been set forth infallibly by the ordinary and universal magisterium.

The Congregation for the Doctrine of the Faith doesn't have the authority to determine which Church teachings are infallible and which aren't. Only a pope speaking *ex cathedra* or an Ecumenical Council of the Bishops can determine this. Now, that wasn't the case. Pope John Paul II had not spoken *ex cathedra*, nor had he said he was teaching infallibly. He had said only it was a 'judgment' that is 'to be definitely held', not a matter of 'divine faith' that must be 'believed'. As for the universal teaching of the world's bishops, they hadn't been consulted on the matter.

Of course, the CDF knew all that, but obviously still wanted the faithful to believe it was infallible and to treat it as such: a classic case of the 'creeping infallibility' or 'pseudo infallibility' which has beleaguered the Church to this day.

It marked an increase in the repression of other views seen as 'dissenting'. The widespread silencing of debate started being enforced brutally. There was spying, delation and reporting of anybody still supporting women's ordination, or even just asking for continuation of the debate. Irish Mercy Sister Carmel McEnroy, Professor of Theology at St

Press briefing with Joan Chittister at Dublin WOW Conference, 2001

Soline at BASIC podium

Pontifical Diploma in Spiritual Guidance

Being interviewed by Joe Little of RTÉ in Rosslare Harbour

With (l-r) Colm's brothers Peter and John, Colm, artist Nora Kelly, Soline and Mary T. Malone; grandmother Martha (106) in front

The Last Supper by Bohdan Piasecki

Soline in Knock

*My long-time supporter,
Eamonn McCarthy*

Soline with stole outside Dublin Procathedral, 2017

March against abuse and cover-up in the Church, Phil Dunne on the right

WOW Eucharist in Termonfeckin

'Priest, why not you?' in Ars, France

Pride march with Ursula Halligan (centre) and Fr Bernárd Lynch (right)

Celebrating the Eucharist with Diarmuid Ua Conáill and Joe Mulvaney

Sister Geneviève's gift to me of paten and chalice

In St Raphael's Garden, Oylegate, County Wexford

With Ursula Halligan, Mary McAleese, Canon Ginnie Kennerley in Christ Church

Why not, indeed? St Thérèse and me

Outside Trinity College chapel

No Woman, No Church march, Dublin Nunciature, 2020

International Women's Day march at the Spire, 2025, with Colm and Maeve Walsh

Meinrad's Seminary in the US, was fired from her post for merely adding her name to an ad in the *National Catholic Reporter* requesting continuing discussion on the issue. On the other hand, opposition to women's ordination, preferably loudly proclaimed, became an essential requirement for clerical advancement and episcopal appointment.

Fear stalked the Church as witch-hunting became rampant. To survive under this form of dictatorship clerics and theologians, or anyone in Church employment (such as teachers in Catholic schools), kept their heads down 'below the parapet'. I used to joke grimly that the parapet had become the dominant church structure. The institutional Church had become a very cold house for women like me. We were to be isolated and frozen out: a form of internal exile in Siberia!

It wasn't just my own pain and suffering through the following decades which was difficult, but also witnessing other women worse affected, and the good men who stood by their consciences here and abroad. Many clerics, religious, theologians and others lost their jobs and ministries and were prevented from teaching, lecturing or publishing.

6.

A Woman at the Altar

In 1995, a Dominican sister returned from a retreat in Knock with a precious gift for me. It was a young child's drawing of a priest at the altar during Mass. What made it special was that the priest was a woman. The picture had been made by a child preparing for Holy Communion and exhibited in Knock. My friend Sister Genevieve was so moved by it she asked if she could have it.

There was no name on it and I have often wondered whether the child inspired to draw it was a girl? Did she feel called to be a priest? Soon after I showed it to Bishop Thomas Flynn of Achonry, who was left speechless. I said: 'The Spirit is speaking to us through the children.'

Of all the places in Ireland there was no more fitting place for this picture of a woman at the altar. After all, isn't Knock a uniquely Marian and Eucharistic shrine where Mary appeared in a priestly role in 1879?

In his analysis of the symbolic message of the apparition, Father Berchmans Walsh from Knock wrote:

> She [Mary] co-offered and still co-offers (on the human plane of course) with the Lamb the supreme sacrifice of merciful love that redeemed and saves us. This is admirably demonstrated by the posture she assumed at Knock, as in no other of her apparitions,

ie praying with her hands extended and raised to the levels of the shoulders – as a priest prays during the Eucharistic prayer of the Mass.

At the same time that picture of a woman at the altar was exhibited in Knock, copies of a book called *Woman at the Altar* by Sister Lavinia Byrne IBVM were being destroyed by its American religious publishers by order of the local bishop. This was as a result of the book being banned by the Congregation for the Doctrine of the Faith.

The book, completed before *Ordinatio Sacerdatolis* but published afterwards in 1994, asserted:

> The ordination of women to the priesthood is the logical conclusion of all the recent work of Catholic Theology about women and, in particular, about the holiness of all the baptised. It is not an aberration from what the Church teaches, but rather a fulfilment of it so that not to ordain women would now be to compromise the catholicity of the Church.

And Lavinia Byrne draws our attention to the image she had specially chosen for the front cover of *Woman at the Altar*:

> [It] shows an extraordinary image, a wonderful representation of Mary from Ravenna. She stands exalted in a deep blue chasuble, with a stole around her neck. She is surrounded by gold mosaic relief, her hands raised in supplication and offering. This too is part of the Catholic tradition and we ignore it at our peril.

It would appear that the child in Knock knew more about the Catholic tradition than the learned and wise men of the Sacred Congregation for the Doctrine of the Faith who banned *A Woman at the Altar*.

ಬ ಬ ಬ

ONE DARK NIGHT IN DECEMBER 1995, I became increasingly depressed. It was so bad that on Christmas day I was unable to go with Colm and the boys to my in-laws for Christmas dinner. However, I did notice an unusual gift around the Christmas tree: A live butterfly fluttering around, a sign of resurrection.

A few days later I was in bed reading Thomas Merton's book *Seeds of Contemplation* when the idea suddenly came to me to celebrate the Eucharist. The oppressive darkness which had enveloped me lifted at once. It was like sunshine dissipating a thick fog. It took me completely by surprise as it hadn't been in my mind, not consciously in any case.

One of the BASIC members from Belfast, Joe Sheehy, had been urging me for several years to start presiding at the Eucharist, but I had always refused.

'What are you waiting for? Permission from Rome? It will never come, they are incapable of it. Are you afraid of being excommunicated?'

To which I would respond: 'No, I am not afraid of being excommunicated, but I don't want to do it as an ego trip. I would want to know it's God asking me to do it. Eucharist is about self-offering, I don't want to be grasping at it.'

Joe would counter, quite reasonably: 'And how will you know?'

'I don't know how I will know, but I will know' is all I could ever reply, much to Joe's exasperation.

So now I was left wondering, is that it? Is God calling me? Or is it just me wanting to do it? Is it a temptation? Or an invitation? Or a commandment? 'Do this in memory of me?' Of course I knew it was against Church law. But Church law didn't factor in women having a say anyway. I was on my own. I wouldn't rush into it. I would take the time to discern what was right.

A few days passed and the idea grew. I had mentioned it to Eamonn who listened. I was at peace. I prayed: 'God, you can ask me anything. I just want to know it's You who are asking me.' Could I ask God for a sign?

And then I got a visit from a friend, a French missionary sister, Geneviève, who was back from Rwanda where she had gone during the genocide to help the victims. When we had first met a few years previously we had both felt it was like the Visitation of Mary and Elisabeth.

Now Geneviève was bringing me a mystery gift, carefully wrapped. As I was opening it, she said: 'It has been a long gestation, but your time has come. Rome is not ready, but you are ready.' I unpacked a beautiful small pottery chalice and paten. I was filled with wonder.

She went on: 'I bought it in France during the summer and brought it back to Rwanda, intending it as a gift for a priest there, but then I got a sense that instead I was to give it to you.'

I told her what I had been pondering in the past few days. 'This is the sign.'

She smiled back. 'Thanks be to God!'

Now I knew. What was particularly moving for me was that the chalice and paten had been made in the region in France where my mother was from.

There remained the question of when I would first celebrate. At first I thought it might be on the first of January, feast of Mary, Mother of God, but I sensed no, it wasn't right. Then it came to me it that it should be Saturday, 6 January, feast of the Epiphany, in the afternoon. I told Eamonn who said he would come. Genevieve couldn't come because of a chapter meeting but said she would be with us in spirit. I also called Joe, a journalist who had been a religious and who, after interviewing me recently, had said, 'If ever you decide to celebrate Mass, could you please invite me?' to which I had replied, 'Eucharist is not by invitation. I will let you know.' So I told Joe, who said he would come.

I was wondering what to do with the children since I didn't feel they should be present, when an invitation came for them to attend a friend's birthday party that afternoon. I could only marvel at how everything was falling into place.

I had bread, I would need wine. I went to the garage where we had some in a cupboard. I picked a bottle at random and read the label: Château Sainte-Marie! I had never seen that wine before but it couldn't have been more fitting: Mary's wine. And of course there was a clear echo of the wedding feast at Cana in John's Gospel: A Eucharistic sign where Mary is the active initiator.

Colm, Eamonn, Joe (three wise men) and myself gathered around our dining room table celebrating the Eucharist on the feast of the Epiphany. I knew in the depths of my being I was doing what I had been born to do. There was no sense of transgressing, just deep peace and joy. I was giving birth to what had been gestating in me for a long time, and in generations of women before me. I was being true to my deepest self, fulfilling my vocation. With God nothing is impossible. *Magnificat*!

⁂

For about 10 years I celebrated Eucharist on weekdays on my own. Like everything else on my spiritual journey, it wasn't planned. It evolved out of that Epiphany Eucharistic celebration in January 1996. Was that to be a once off? What was I to do with that chalice and paten gifted to me? Put them away?

Gradually it came to me to celebrate Eucharist on my own on weekdays. On Sundays we would continue going to Mass in a parish church. Celebrating on my own wasn't what I would have preferred, but it was all that was possible, given the circumstances at the time.

Of course, I did question what I was doing in terms of underlying theology. The Eucharist is by its very nature a community celebration. So was I not on shaky ground by celebrating alone? How could I justify it? The reality was that everything I did was on shaky ground, a bit like walking on water.

But what I discovered as I celebrated Eucharist day after day was that I became increasingly aware of the cosmic dimension and the Communion of Saints. While there was no visible congregation present, I was far from alone. I sensed the presence of a multitude. I was praying with the angels and the saints and the whole Church. It was not a private solitary ritual; it was with, and for, the whole world.

I wondered how long I would be celebrating on my own, and I never thought I would be doing it for ten years. I certainly never imagined I would some day be filmed doing it! When I look back on that time, I see it was like manna in the desert: A strange and unusual food, but one that nourished me day by day. It kept my vocation alive.

ಬಿ ಬಿ ಬಿ

IN THE SUMMER OF 1996, A FEW weeks before my fortieth birthday, I suddenly felt a strong desire to spend it in Lourdes. That meant cancelling a hotel booking in Connemara and searching for flight and hotel at short notice. Colm performed this minor miracle to get us a three days' stay.

Colm and I had never been to Lourdes before. I remembered my father saying, when my mother was very ill, that we would all go there as a family if she recovered. As she hadn't survived, we never went. I now felt there was some unfinished business. While she hadn't been cured her suffering had ended and she was now enjoying eternal life. Lourdes was calling me. We arrived in early August with a group of Irish pilgrims and a priest chaplain.

We immersed ourselves in pilgrim life in Lourdes. Colm declined going to the baths, even though the queue was considerably shorter for the men than for the women. I joined the long queue anyway and recited the Rosary while waiting for the different intentions, which were called out. When my turn finally came, I heard the intention being called as I entered the baths: 'For vocations to the priesthood' and I smiled to myself.

I had no special expectation concerning the baths. I just knew it was one of the main rituals for pilgrims. The only thing I expected was that it would be cold, and probably not very pleasant.

The attendants helped me into the water. What I then experienced I can only describe as being immersed in liquid joy. As I was standing up to get out the attendants reproached me that I hadn't said the prayer which was posted on the wall. How could I explain that I was praying with my whole being? I did read out the words, though they fell far short of describing the joy I felt.

When I came out and re-joined Colm I was still glowing. It was pure gift. Sunday was our last day and my actual birthday. We went to Mass in the underground basilica, which was absolutely filled.

Around the altar were dozens of bishops and perhaps two hundred priests. When the time for Communion came, Colm and I joined one of the many queues. Ours was long, but I remember thinking, 'at least it's not like the January sales in the shops, they won't have run out by the time we reach the top'. But then I saw the Ministers of the Eucharist being recalled to the altar while there were still half a dozen people in front of us.

We made our way back to our seats, empty handed. I was absolutely stunned. I had been a steward in the Phoenix Park during the Papal Mass and along with everybody else had received. The Mass continued normally. There was no announcement to explain why the distribution of Communion had been cut short. The mitres were put back on and all the clergy processed out in great solemnity.

Colm was resigned to what had happened. I was not. I could not believe Christ had called me to Lourdes for my fortieth birthday to be deprived of the Eucharist. It was particularly ironic as the Gospel of the day was the Multiplication of the Loaves and Fishes, with everyone being fed!

Instead, here the clergy had helped themselves first and turned away some of us.

I thought of the pain of those who are deprived of the Eucharist, not once, but permanently, because they don't comply with the rules, like those who remarried after divorce. Everybody was now filing out of the basilica.

'I am not leaving without receiving. I haven't come all the way for this,' I told Colm. We saw a priest still in vestments at the door, so I explained to him what had happened. For good measure, I added that it was the feast day of St John Vianney, patron saint of priests, and that he would not have left his parishioners without the Eucharist.

The priest then brought us to a tabernacle from which he took out a large ciborium filled to the brim, from which he gave us Communion. I could see others, equally full. What was the point of having these under lock and key and depriving some people? As I prayed after receiving Communion, I decided it was a sign of the Eucharistic famine worldwide, a famine of Love.

Our pilgrimage in Lourdes was to finish with lunch at the hotel before departing to the airport. As I sat down at table I was still pondering the events of the morning, when the chaplain mentioned that one of the bishops present at the Mass was the Archbishop of Tuam, Michael Neary, and I made a note of it.

The conversation then took an ugly turn as the priest, for no obvious reason, started making derogatory statements about women priests. I kept my head down and said nothing, but when he referred to the Anglican Church as 'a zoo' I couldn't let it pass as there were no Anglicans among us to defend themselves.

I said, 'The Anglicans are our brothers and sisters in Christ, not animals.' The priest then attacked me verbally to the point we wondered if he might hit me. It had all turned very sour.

This was my fortieth birthday lunch but I could hardly swallow my food at that stage, as all that bile had been dumped on me. I finished my meal and felt the need to go to the Blessed Sacrament chapel. There I regained a measure of peace as I prayed for that priest who was obviously a deeply unhappy and troubled man.

Back in Dublin I wrote to Archbishop Neary to let him know what had happened at the Mass at which he had been a chief presider. A reply came from his secretary informing me that the archbishop had been unaware of the Lourdes incident, but is acutely conscious of the 'Eucharistic Famine'. He is absolutely determined to dedicate his episcopate to the relief of that hunger.

When I later shared this incident with friends, their response was, 'It had to happen to you!' Well, it certainly contributed to making my fortieth birthday truly memorable, although not in the way I had imagined.

ಬ ಬ ಬ

NOW THAT CARDINAL DALY WAS ABOUT to retire, his successor, Seán Brady, was appointed as coadjutor bishop. In an interview for *Reality* magazine, he was asked whether he would meet with people in the Church who felt alienated, such as women. He said he would. That positive statement spurred me to write asking for a meeting. I specified I had already met with his predecessor and with my own archbishop in Dublin. I waited for months but no response came.

Then it was time for the National Conference of Priests of Ireland to hold their public gathering. I decided to attend, as I had done previously a few times. In the weeks before the gathering, a passage from John's Gospel kept popping into my mind: Jesus talking with the Samaritan woman at the well. I reflected that if there was an opportunity at the NCPI, I would say: 'If Jesus could dialogue with a Samaritan woman, why do churchmen refuse to give women like me a hearing?'

The gathering in September 1996, in All Hallows, was to start with a plenary meeting with Archbishop Seán Brady as speaker. This was his first time addressing the NCPI since being selected by Rome to become Primate of All Ireland. There was dinner being served beforehand. As I was having a cup of tea in the packed dining room a professional photographer approached and asked me and a couple beside me whether we would be willing to be photographed with the archbishop for the *Cork Examiner*.

Now that was a surprise! We agreed and we were led outdoors. We had a very brief chat with the archbishop while we were being lined up for the photos. I was wearing a name badge and mentioned my name, but that didn't seem to ring any bells with him.

After that there was a bit of time before the public talk and I found myself alone in the middle of a long corridor when Seán Brady came in the opposite direction. There were just the two us. I thought, when that photo is published tomorrow the penny will have dropped as to who I am. He will think he was tricked, that somehow I arranged to be photographed with him to embarrass him, or that the photographer did. So I told him, 'I don't think you realise who I am. I want you to know I was asked by the photographer and he didn't know, he usually covers sport, not Church matters.'

He blanched: 'I know who you are, I have your letter on my desk.'

I nodded. He didn't say anything more, just moved on.

A few minutes later, in a hall packed to capacity, I listened to Seán Brady give an eloquent plea for dialogue, referring especially to the situation in the North. He quoted Scripture only once: 'When Jesus crossed the religious sectarian divide to speak with the Samaritan woman he unleashed fresh energy for change and transformation.' I couldn't believe my ears. It was as if a signal had been given to me.

Seán Brady ended his talk to loud applause and then it was time for questions. Surprisingly there was a long silence with nobody rushing in. I hadn't planned to speak but the Samaritan woman was prodding me with a sharp finger. My heart beating loudly I plucked up my courage and stood up. I quoted back what Seán Brady had just said about Jesus and the Samaritan woman and went on: 'Would the archbishop be willing to meet me and other women called to the priesthood, or are we less than the Samaritan woman?' I also added that he may wish to answer me privately afterwards.

But no. Seán Brady decided he would answer publicly and abruptly: 'No, the pope has spoken.'

His answer, in tone and content, couldn't have been more at odds with the speech he had just delivered. There was a long, shocked silence.

The image I had was that of a beautiful soufflé dish rising in the oven and then collapsing. There followed some questions, but the atmosphere in the hall had changed. When it was over, many people made a point of telling me how sorry they were for how I had been treated. One of them was Garret Fitzgerald, our former Taoiseach.

We went for a wine and cheese reception. I was still trembling, but seeing Seán Brady flanked by two fellow clerics I approached him: 'I still believe it would be good if we could meet sometime and talk to each other.'

'Now I have met you,' he replied glacially. It was final. I was dismissed. I could sense his anger and that of his companions. And perhaps even fear? These tall, powerful men being confronted by a small, persistent woman.

The following morning the *Cork Examiner* newspaper carried an article headlined: 'Call For Dialogue In Church To Heal The Hurt Of Those Who Feel Alienated.'

The archbishop was quoted as saying, 'If we do not engage in real dialogue, the people will just walk away and will be alienated.' And above it was a nice photo of me smiling beside him in the sunshine!

I heard later some priests felt I had acted terribly for embarrassing the new archbishop. Did they know the archbishop had said in *Reality* that he would meet with women alienated in the Church? Did they know that after nine months he still hadn't replied to my letter?

There was a report in *The Furrow* about the Conference. The young priest who wrote it told me, decades afterwards, that he got complaints for mentioning my public exchange with the archbishop and not making him look good.

Instead, they should have blamed Jesus and the Samaritan woman!

ಬಿ ಬಿ ಬಿ

NOT BEING BELIEVED IS THE ONE THING I have found most painful. One morning I was in the Church of St Thérèse in Mount Merrion, pouring my heart out before the Blessed Sacrament: 'They don't believe me, send somebody else with that message, or tell them yourself.' There was no answer, but at least I had vented my frustration.

I left the church and started walking in the park nearby. There I met an older man. I greeted him and picking up on my French accent he asked me what I was doing around here. I decided I might as well be direct about my sense of vocation, at the risk of shocking him. He wasn't shocked, he was very interested.

He introduced himself as John P. Duggan, a retired lieutenant colonel. As we strolled on, it was his turn to surprise me: 'Would you agree to give a talk to the Knights of Columbanus about it?'

I laughed in disbelief: 'The Knights of Columbanus? You must be joking! I really don't think they'd want to hear me.'

The Knights of Columbanus is a conservative, Catholic all-male organisation. But he was serious: 'I am a member of the Knights, I'll try and organise for you to speak at a meeting.'

I was dumbfounded. I then told him I had just complained to the Blessed Sacrament about not being believed, and now here he was, not only believing me but wanting me to speak to the Knights! I had to take back my complaint.

I must confess that as we parted, I still thought it unlikely that I would be invited to speak to the Knights. But I was wrong. Several months later John called me to say it was agreed. 'God bless your powers of persuasion,' is all I could say.

When the day came, John collected me in the evening and drove us to Ely Place, the headquarters of the Knights. Inside they were all men, apart from the wife of one of the members, who had got special permission to attend because I was speaking. The priest chaplain was in attendance.

After a brief introduction it was my turn to speak. I started by quoting St Bernadette's words to her parish priest in Lourdes: 'I have only been asked to tell you, not to convince you.' I then shared an outline of my vocational journey.

They were attentive, and at the end there was courteous applause. There were a few questions, and then a relaxed cup of tea. I don't know what they made of my talk, but there was courtesy and openness as they gave me a hearing. After this rather surreal evening my friendship with John Duggan developed, along with his support, until his death in 2013. To John, the army man, I was Joan of Arc!

ಬ ಬ ಬ

IN 1995 ARCHBISHOP CONNELL HAD announced he was going to take up a proposal from the Dublin Diocesan Council of Priests to set up a forum for women to dialogue with the archbishop, bishops and Council of Priests on issues of common concern.

I attended the Women's Forum's meetings in my local parish of Blackrock, and in March 1997 was elected to replace one the parish representatives who had stepped down. This meant attending the Forum deanery meetings and also some diocesan ones in Clonliffe. But the atmosphere deteriorated as efforts at censoring increased, trust was damaged (yet again!) and I resigned at the end of 1997, not one day too soon, in utter frustration.

A report was presented to the archbishop, who requested it be re-written because it had one sentence on the ordination of women. The issue had been brought up in a number of parishes and the women who wrote the report rightly felt that if it was omitted it would not represent what the women of the diocese had said. Credibility was at stake.

A few years later a document was produced, but was so watered down that it was more on the role of the laity than on women and inclusiveness. I wasn't the only woman who felt let down by the Women's Forum, despite the brave and unstinting work of some of its leaders. Many left burnt out and disillusioned. In the diocese it became a byword for a 'failed effort'.

One small incident remains with me, indicative of the underlying misogyny. The women in my parish had expressed the desire to invite the priests to one of the Forum meetings. As Forum representative I mentioned this to our curate, saying he would be very welcome. I can still hear his acerbic reply: 'Why would I go into that den of vipers? No thanks!'

I didn't have the heart to report back to the women, who were among the most dedicated supporters of the parish, what their priest thought of them. He may have called us vipers, but all the venom was on his tongue.

༒   ༒   ༒

IN TRUTH, THE ISSUE OF WOMEN PRIESTS was not something which was welcome by all women, far from it. I had my eyes opened to the extent that many saw themselves as unfit, somehow inferior or not deserving.

On one of the first radio interviews I did I was joined by Alice Glenn, a formidable woman twice my age who had until recently been a TD. She was a very outspoken politician and a staunch traditional Catholic. She was not only opposed to women's ordination, but when I mentioned women doing readings at Mass she immediately countered: 'As a woman I could never do that, I am not worthy to stand in the sanctuary.'

I told her: 'Mary and the female disciples were at the foot of the Cross, so why would women not be worthy to be near the altar?'

She looked at me as if she had never thought about that, but I could see she could not shake off decades of prohibitions and indoctrination.

On another occasion a woman telephoned me in great anguish: 'How could I want to be a priest? We, women, should be repenting in humility for the sin of Eve, not coveting the dignity of the priesthood.' Nothing I could say would change her mind that women were on earth to do penance for belonging to the sex which had brought sin into the world.

Besides these distorted religious views there was plain misogyny and sexism. One of the most surprising examples came from a well-known Catholic journalist who in her youth had been involved with the women's liberation movement. In one of her newspaper columns she argued against women priests on the grounds that women couldn't be trusted to keep secrets, so how could you go to a woman for confession? And secondly, women are only interested in fashion, so imagine how they would just want fancy vestments, and so on?

It was such a gross caricature it would have been laughable, but she was writing in earnest. She obviously had bought into a very negative view of her gender. How many others were the same?

The more encounters I had, the more I realised how centuries of being treated as inferior, second class and subordinate had affected women, especially when this sexism had been justified as the will of God Himself. For God, of course, was always He, or 'the man above', as God was colloquially referred to, an expression which always made me wince. The God I believed in and loved was definitely not 'the man above'!

ಜ ಜ ಜ

MY WORK FOR WOMEN'S ORDINATION only increased my commitment to Church unity and reconciliation. I joined the North Wicklow Ecumenical Group for priests and ministers and later became a member of the Decem, a longstanding ecumenical, male-only clergy group – that is, until they graciously admitted me and other women.

Still, it was a surprise when in the Spring of 1997 I received an invitation from a Decem member and Church of Ireland rector, Jim Carroll, asking if I would preach at three services on Sunday, 20 April? I readily agreed.

As I checked the calendar I realised it was Vocations Sunday in the Roman Catholic Church. I thought the Holy Spirit had a sense of humour. It was the right day for me to fulfil my vocation. The irony of course was that I had received permission to preach from the Church of Ireland Archbishop of Dublin, Walton Empey. I would never have received such permission to preach at Mass in my own Church.

I arrived early at All Saints, Raheny, on a bright sunny morning, with all the joy, fervour and trepidation of a first Communicant. Well, it was my first time preaching. I had prepared, but had not written down a text.

The rector introduced me to the congregation and invited me to proclaim the Gospel from John 10, 'I am the Good Shepherd'. Even to be able to proclaim the Gospel in a church was a first for me and moved me deeply. I then preached. And then again at the next service, and later on in St John the Evangelist, Coolock.

What was particularly poignant is that my father-in-law was the son of a 'mixed marriage'. He had been brought up Roman Catholic like his mother, while his father was a member of the Church of Ireland. When his father had died he had been advised not to go to the funeral, as it was considered a sin for a Catholic to attend a service in a Protestant church. He and his mother had ignored the rule, but there was an abyss between the two denominations.

I was very aware of this family history as I preached on 'There will be one flock, since there is one Shepherd' (John 10:16) and I told the story. I felt I was bridging the division in my own small way. As I drove home afterwards I was filled with a deep sense of fulfilment, of hope and above all gratitude: to God who made it possible and to the people who welcomed me with such kindness.

Bishop Willie Walsh of Killaloe had just apologised for these unChristian, unloving rules which caused so much pain to so many people. I had then written to him asking: 'What are the current Church regulations for which the bishops will be apologising in twenty years' time because they are unChristian and unloving?'

℘ ℘ ℘

WITH MY STRONG ECUMENICAL commitment it was only natural that I would be asked frequently, 'Why don't you join another Christian denomination which ordains women?'

It is a question I asked myself when I first became aware of my calling to ordained ministry in the mid-1970s. If the church I belonged to didn't want me as a priest/minister, could I follow my calling in another one, and should I?

The issue of joining another denomination became more persistent after 1990. My own sense of vocation was now so strong it had to find expression. The Catholic Church was still closed but the Anglican Church, the Church of Ireland, had started ordaining women, and of course they had married clergy. One of the first women ordained was Ginnie Kennerley, with whom I had studied in the Irish School of Ecumenics.

After *Ordinatio Sacerdatolis* in 1994 and the increasing repression, the issue of joining the Church of Ireland became very live. I knew several Catholic women had made or were making that move. I had a meeting with the woman in charge of vocations in the Church of Ireland, who herself had been a Catholic before being ordained. It was a helpful conversation, as we both determined it wasn't where I was called. The Church of Ireland just wasn't my spiritual 'home'.

A chance encounter also made me reflect about changing denominations. While standing in Grafton Street in Dublin gathering petitions for the ordination of women, I had a brief chat with an American visitor. She had been Roman Catholic, but had joined the Presbyterian church where she was now ordained. As she put it, 'I took my marbles and went to play somewhere else'. What struck me as she spoke was how angry and bitter she still was that she had to leave. Her ordination in the Presbyterian church didn't seem to have given her any peace or joy. So much so that I wondered how she could possibly minister in her new denomination while being in such a negative frame of mind.

After our exchange I thought: What would it profit me to be ordained in another church if I carried around that kind of hurt of rejection? It would poison me and everybody around me. Changing denominations to be ordained was not an automatic solution, a panacea.

Clearly, there were women (as well as men) who have moved and it was right for them. They can flourish and have a fruitful ministry. But again, there isn't one path for everybody.

Surprisingly, or perhaps not, many who suggested that I should leave to be ordained elsewhere have been Roman Catholics, often clergy, wanting to preserve the status quo. 'If you want to be ordained, you can just go and join the

Church of Ireland!' Which meant, get lost, join the Protestants, and leave us in peace! That way nothing would have to change.

Later the idea of being ordained as an inter-faith minister presented itself, as some women I know have opted for that path, including the well known singer and theologian Nóirín Ní Riain. With my interest in other faiths, I thought about it very seriously, but again decided it wasn't for me.

ಬಿ ಬಿ ಬಿ

THERE WAS NO END TO THE BAD NEWS coming from Rome. As some people still dared to express strong doubts about this so-called 'infallible doctrine', and the paucity of its reasonable arguments, more had to be done to enforce obedience. In June 1998, Pope John Paul II issued *At Tuendam Fidem*. The title said it all: 'To defend the faith.'

It was a strange feeling to realise I was viewed as one of those attackers from whom the faith had to be defended. I didn't believe for a minute I was attacking the faith, but it clearly was how the pope and the Curia saw me and others who advocated for women's ordination: dangerous enemies who would harm the faith. Not faithful, but faith-less.

Hoping for complete silence on the question of women's ordination, Cardinal Ratzinger of the CDF provided a commentary on *Ad Tuendam Fidem* which included the judgment that those who still hold women can be ordained priests are 'no longer in full communion with the Catholic Church'. No longer in full communion. Half way out the door, not quite excommunicated yet, but . . .

There was now a new profession of faith, an oath of fidelity for Catholic theologians and others entering Church offices. This introduced a novel element: In addition to a firm faith in the word of God and everything proposed by the Church as divinely revealed, it added the declaration, 'I also firmly accept and hold each and everything definitely proposed by the Church regarding teaching in faith and morals.' The gag was being tightened.

In Ireland, Eamonn McCarthy was one of the first, if not the first, to be sanctioned. He was due to be appointed parish priest in 1999, but because he refused in conscience to swear this new oath (even with 'mental reservation' in time-honoured fashion), he was unable to take up this office. He has remained a curate to this day.

The Church landscape was now settling under a thick layer of ice, the Second Vatican Council's promise of a new springtime for the Church a distant memory. My older friends who had lived through it remembered the hope of those days with nostalgia.

~ ~ ~

WHILE THE VATICAN COULD TRY TO FREEZE the status quo, it couldn't freeze what was being conceived in the womb of prophetic imagination. For many people, the image of the Last Supper with men only, as depicted by Da Vinci and others, constituted a blockage to imagining women presiding at the Eucharist.

To remedy this, BASIC commissioned a renowned Polish artist, Bohdan Piasecki, to paint the Last Supper as a Jewish Passover, with Mary and the female disciples, and some children, present. Sister Joan Chittister OSB wrote a very good review, but there was still the issue of bringing the painting to the attention of a wider public. We thought

The Late Late Show on RTÉ would be ideal, but they weren't showing any interest despite repeated enquiries.

In early September I went to see the Dublin auxiliary bishop, Dermot O'Mahony, with whom I had shared my sense of vocation. I wanted to tell him I had started presiding at Eucharist, and how it had come about. He showed no surprise. In fact, I was the one surprised when he told me women in Ireland had already done it for the past ten years. That was news to me!

He then asked me: 'Do you believe you will be ordained?'

I replied, 'Yes' and added, 'because my mother has given her life for it'.

As these words passed my own lips, I was astonished as that thought had never crossed my mind. I wondered did I really believe this, and where did that belief come from? The bishop didn't question me any further, but I pondered my answer all the way home. How did I know my mother would even be in favour of women priests? Honestly, I had no rational ground to make the claim I had made.

A few weeks later was the thirtieth anniversary of my mother's death. It was a beautiful autumn day and I decided to spend it remembering her with a solitary hike in Glendalough. Her memory and the sense of her presence filled me with joy.

When I came home, there was a recording on the answering machine from a researcher at *The Late Late Show*. Could they come and see that painting we had told them about months beforehand?

Colm was working in Poland for the week so I had to handle it by myself. The following day, I showed the researcher the painting, pointing out some of its features when, turning to me, she said, 'This seems to matter to you personally very much. Why?'

I told her about my call to the priesthood. She listened and then said, 'Would you be prepared to come on *The Late Late Show* and talk about your vocation? You could bring the painting too.'

I was completely taken by surprise, especially when she added, 'It could be this weekend.'

She explained that there was a strong possibility of a cancellation and that a slot would be available. She would confirm it with me and check to get my answer. She had seen my hesitation: 'You won't get another opportunity.'

Confirmation came the following day: Meryl Streep had had to withdraw. I would be taking her slot!

Colm wasn't expected to be home until very late and would have missed the programme, but an unexpected change in business plans freed him so that he could be in the audience.

I had a long wait in the Green room waiting my turn, but I had no nerves at all, which was a blessing. The host, Gay Byrne, was quite curious, although patronising, about this young French wife and mother who wanted to be a Catholic priest, but I was able to answer all his questions, and the Last Supper painting was on display.

What the nation made of it all, I don't know. There was very little feedback. But it was an important step forward for me. That was the week of my mother's thirtieth anniversary. Did she have a hand in it? I believe so.

AFTER CARDINAL DALY'S REFUSAL TO accept the petition, the collecting of signatures continued until we reached over 20,000. Since they were all hand-written, it was quite an impressive pile which had accumulated as months and years passed by. They came from all corners of the country, and represented the efforts, and hopes, of people of all ages who had signed them. The petition had also helped to keep discussion of the issue alive, in spite of the official silencing.

In spring 1999, we decided it was time to deliver them and that the Irish bishops were the ones who should receive them. For me, it was not just a task but an important action, as that petition had sprung six years earlier from deep within me and had brought BASIC into life.

I decided I would do this on my mother's birthday, 21 April. I carefully divided the petitions into 26 bundles, tied a purple ribbon around each, and enclosed them in large envelopes addressed to each bishop, together with a covering letter. I was grateful for all who had gathered that harvest of names, and prayed that they find open hearts and minds. I then brought the bulky load to the Post Office, where the staff were curious what it was all about! I had a great sense of 'mission accomplished' with the petition now out of my hands.

To the great surprise of the country, the following day the singer Sinéad O'Connor was ordained a priest in the Latin Tridentine Church in a private ceremony in Lourdes. It made headline news, putting the spotlight on the exclusion of women from the priesthood, albeit from a rather 'sensational' angle!

A Divine Calling

What the Irish bishops made of that synchronicity we'll never know. Only a few had the courtesy to acknowledge receipt of the petition.

ಲಾ   ಲಾ   ಲಾ

I STILL HAD A DESIRE TO TRY TO MEET with Pope John Paul II. Colm, who was spending a lot of time in Poland for work, heard that there was a priest who was a close friend of the pope who might be able to help me. A meeting was arranged.

I flew out in early December 1999 to Warsaw. It was a physically painful journey because I had hurt my back shortly beforehand. I travelled with a biography of the pope, but found the thick volume more useful as an extra back support. In wintery Warsaw I met up with Colm and a Polish colleague, and we headed to Krakow by train. I wondered whether my back would survive the train journey and walking on the slippery, snow-covered cobblestones.

It was a relief to reach the house of the Polish priest. He received us and listened to my story which a colleague translated. The priest, Mieczyslaw Malinski, had been a friend with Karol Wojtyla in the underground seminary. He was not shocked by my sense of vocation. He was a theologian and had studied in Germany under Karl Rahner, and obviously was open to the possibility. But he felt that the pope, who was turned towards the East and the Orthodox Church, could not move in that direction.

He agreed to pass on a message and my recorded testimony the next time he went to Rome, although he couldn't say when that would be. He then gave me a dedicated copy of his own book of reflections, *Keep Loving*. As we returned from Krakow we discussed our meeting. I already knew that nothing would come of it, but I felt it had to be attempted.

On 8 December, the feast of the Immaculate Conception of Mary, I went to Mass in one of Warsaw's churches. It was overflowing with people and there were several priests on the altar. I was fascinated by their chasubles decorated with beautiful images of Mary. I reflected that these men could wear her image, but they would not let her or any woman near the altar!

Later, at a dinner with business colleagues, one of the Polish men observed, 'Here, in Poland, we have many clerics, but very few priests'. He understood the difference. That sentence has stayed with me though one could add, not just in Poland.

I never heard again from Monsignor Malinski, which didn't surprise me. What did surprise me was to read in *The Tablet* in the summer of 2007 that he was named as one of the many clerics who had collaborated with the secret police during the communist regime, informing on Karol Wojtyla under the code name Delta. He admitted contacts but denied he was a spy.

ʛ ʛ ʛ

I HAVE HAD A STRONG DEVOTION to the Sacred Heart for many years and have visited Paray-le-Monial in France several times. One of my favourite prayers to the Sacred Heart is its French version, with its familiar 'tu':

> *Coeur Sacré de Jesus j'ai confiance en Toi.*
> *Coeur Sacré de Jésus, je confie le passé à ta miséricorde, le présent à ton amour et l' avenir à ta providence.*

> Sacred Heart of Jesus I trust in You. Sacred Heart of Jesus I entrust the past to your mercy, the present to your love and the future to your providence.

I cannot recall when I first acquired this devotion. Perhaps it was through my maternal grandmother? She had small embroidered pictures of Jesus showing his heart, with the words:

'Voilà le coeur qui a tant aimé les hommes'
('This the Heart which has loved wo/men so much').

But there was no picture of the Sacred Heart on the wall at home. It was therefore a novelty to me when I discovered pictures of the Sacred Heart in Irish homes. They were fairly common in 1969, and the little red light in front of them reminded me of the sanctuary light before the Blessed Sacrament.

I knew that Jesus had given his Heart to some of the saints. I still have a small picture of the Sacred Heart my good friend Madeleine Sophie, a religious of the Sacred Heart, had given me, inscribed with the words, 'My Heart is yours'.

I prayed but did not expect a response, it was all so spontaneous, but the response I got was, 'If I give you my Heart, with what shall I love you?'

I had no ready answer to that question, but the inner voice added, 'I will give you my Mother's Heart.'

It was a brief silent prayer dialogue but it marked me deeply. I had no doubt then or since of the reality of the gift of Mary's Heart.

7.

Women's Ordination Worldwide

We do not choose saints, they choose us! St Thérèse didn't show up into my life until I was in my thirties, until I needed her and was ready to receive her help.

I knew of her as St Thérèse of Lisieux, or St Thérèse of the Child Jesus, or the Little St Thérèse, but what little I knew didn't appeal to me. I saw a lot of statues of her in French churches and to me that's exactly what she was, a plaster saint. We didn't call her 'the Little flower' in France, but there was a lot of sickly sweet stuff sticking to the pious images representing her. She appeared quite unreal. I could not relate to her.

All that changed on a ferry crossing to France for our summer holidays in July 1991. I had taken the latest bulletin of the *St Joan's Alliance* to read on board and discovered an article by a priest mentioning that St Thérèse had a deep, lasting desire to be a priest. Now that was news!

As we were crossing Normandy we stopped off in Lisieux. That was my first visit and the beginning of a relationship with Thérèse. There were many more pilgrimages to Lisieux and the more I read about her, the more I discovered the complex person she had been beneath the simplistic edited versions of her life. Of special interest was what didn't appear in any biography, which was the surprising ways she had expressed her desire to be a priest, as described in *St Thérèse of Lisieux by Those Who Knew Her* (edited by Christopher O'Mahony). According to Sister Genevieve of Saint Teresa OCD:

> In 1897, but before she was really ill, Sister Thérèse told me she expected to die that year. Here is the reason she gave me for this in June. When she realised that she had pulmonary tuberculosis, she said: 'You see, God is going to take me at an age when I would not have had the time to become a priest... If I could have been a priest, I would have been ordained at these June ordinations. So, what did God do? So that I would not be disappointed, he let me be sick: in that way I couldn't have been there, and I would die before I could exercise my ministry.
>
> The sacrifice of not being able to be a priest was something she always felt deeply. During her illness, whenever cutting her hair, she would ask for a tonsure, and then joyfully feel it with her hand. But her regret did not find its expression merely in such trifles; it was caused by a real love of God, and inspired high hopes in her.

In 2001 the relics of St Thérèse came to Ireland. Several members of BASIC decided to go to Rosslare with the aim of highlighting her desire to be a priest. We lined the road to the harbour with placards of her photo inscribed 'Welcome Saint Thérèse, Called to be a Priest'. As the boat was delayed the RTÉ crew had time for Religious & Social Affairs Correspondent Joe Little to interview us.

To our surprise we featured that evening on RTÉ television news, together with a brief interview with Bishop Brendan Comiskey who confirmed that her vocation to the priesthood was well documented. Well documented, but also kept well hidden from the faithful! Since then St Thérèse has been adopted by the International Movement for Women's Ordination.

In late July 2006, I was pouring out my pain in my journal. I wrote: 'I have such a strong desire to be ordained, and in Knock of all places! If it is not your desire, remove it from my heart. But if it is, bring it to fulfilment.'

A letter then dropped through the letter box from my aunt in France. As I opened it, a silver medal fell out depicting a host above a chalice! I sat down to read the letter:

> I didn't know what to send you for your 50th birthday and then I thought you would like this medal which your grand-father got for his first Holy Communion, and which was blessed by the Bishop of Lisieux, Mgr Lemonnier, a relative of the family.

That was the same bishop who had presided at the beatification process and would have heard first hand the sworn testimony that Thérèse wanted to be a priest.

I read the letter a few times. It would have been special to receive this gift at any time, but I was amazed at the timing. A week later, on my fiftiethth birthday, I drove with Eamonn McCarthy to Knock where my vocation had been first blessed and where I had placed it in Mary's heart. It was a day of thanksgiving for the past and of renewed trust for the future.

BASIC HAD BECOME A MEMBER of the new umbrella group Women's Ordination Worldwide. Diarmuid Ua Connail and myself were representing BASIC at a meeting in London when it was decided to hold an international conference on the ordination of women in June 2001. Where would we have it? Diarmuid offered Ireland as the venue, which was readily accepted by the other groups.

I was more reticent. Ours was one of the smallest groups; would we be able to organise it? Diarmuid had experience organising professional conferences and was confident we could manage it. Back in Dublin, the rest of the core group endorsed his view. Now the hard work would start.

The preparation was fraught, with obstacles at every turn. The foot and mouth disease had infected Ireland, so to avoid spreading the disease large gatherings, including St Patrick's Day celebrations, were cancelled. Would Ireland re-open in time? Participants coming from abroad needed to know to make their arrangements.

When that crisis cleared, a new one erupted with the accommodation. We had reserved rooms for participants in University College Dublin where the conference was being held. UCD now informed us there were no rooms available and they had no record of our reservation. Perhaps they had double-booked, but incompetence or conspiracy?

I knew this would mean the end of the conference as we absolutely had to get those rooms. Joan of Arc could take back whole cities, all I needed was a few rooms I reminded myself on my way to the meeting with UCD officials. Eamonn McCarthy still reminds me how I 'drilled' into them. It must have worked. The rooms miraculously became available. If that battle had been won, there were plenty more to come and I would have to beat a path to that office again and again. The UCD computer system seemed incapable of retaining the individual bookings. I received endless complaints from worried participants, and each room had to be nailed down.

The worst was yet to come. In Ireland the Church authorities remained strangely silent about the forthcoming conference. The expectation must have been that it wouldn't take place, that Rome would successfully 'kill' it. Well, they nearly did.

While all was quiet in Dublin, behind the scenes the Vatican was busy trying to decapitate the conference. First was the threat of excommunication hanging over our keynote speaker from the US, Benedictine Sister Joan Chittister, who was also experiencing health problems. Would she be able to come?

Then we heard that the same threat had been made to Sister Myra Poole in the UK. Myra Poole was WOW's main organiser for bursaries and visas for participants from Africa and had crucial contacts. Under huge pressure from the Vatican, and no support from her order, she had to stop her work for the conference.

By now we could see we were facing a massive headwind. It was not just a question of a small committee of volunteers on a shoestring budget, but it was about facing down the might, and wrath, of a patriarchal clerical system intent on stopping the conference from going ahead.

Aruna Gnanadason of the World Council of Churches (WCC) was due to be our opening speaker. She was not Roman Catholic, so at least she would be safe we reckoned.

We were wrong. With only a few weeks to go Aruna informed us she would not be coming with no reason given. She had already sent us a copy of her speech.

We heard afterwards she was the victim of the same kind of bullying. The Vatican is not a full member of the WCC, but it put pressure on it to stop her coming by threatening to withdraw from the WCC Faith and Order Commission of which it was a member. Not only was Aruna pressured not to speak at the conference, but she was also prevented from telling us why.

Now we had to find an opening speaker, and were fortunate to get Rose Hudson Wilkins, an Anglican priest originally from Jamaica, to agree at short notice. She delivered a wonderful speech, and we also distributed copies of Aruna's intended speech, so the Vatican failed to silence us. The Vatican had wanted to collapse the conference quietly, but their bullying tactics only drew more publicity.

I was spokesperson for the conference and as it drew near the international media attention increased dramatically, despite the efforts of the Vatican. It was important but exhausting work as the telephone rang almost nonstop and journalists and photographers called to the door. I had one disquieting interview when an Irish journalist asked me how did I know I wasn't doing the work of the devil? I felt this was more inquisition than journalism.

Besides the Vatican's big guns, there were also anonymous threats of violence at the conference. One letter, which we reported to the Gardaí, was so concerning we had to engage extra private security to protect the speakers.

By the time the conference opened in the O'Reilly Hall in UCD at the end of June, I was exhausted. I realised how tired I was when I stood up to start the conference and couldn't see the big candle right in front of me that was to be lit!

The conference went well, the WOW and BASIC committee members did extraordinary work, as did many volunteers. There was considerable goodwill from the participants from all parts of the globe.

The first two days were overshadowed with worry over Sister Myra Poole. She had arrived in Dublin, but had not attended the conference as she had been threatened by Church authorities that all hell would break loose if she put one foot inside the O'Reilly Hall. I was worried about Myra's state of mind, knowing the terrible pressure she had been under, so was enormously relieved when she finally stepped into the conference to meet with the participants.

By the time the conference was over I was ready to collapse, but there were still things to wrap up, correspondence and a few interviews, including one where I needed to go to Belfast. I travelled on the train and arrived in a deserted hotel. It was coming up to the twelfth of July (the annual Unionist celebration of the Battle of the Boyne) and not a time for tourists! I had been there previously as a guest of Father Gerry Reynolds and the Redemptorists in Clonard monastery, but never at that time of the year.

That night I read a book given to me by some American members of the Women's Ordination Conference, *Out of the Depths*, by Sister Miriam Thérèse Winter. It was the remarkable story of Ludmilla Javarova, a Catholic woman who was ordained a priest in what was then Czechoslovakia when the Church was underground because of communist persecution. I read it deep into the night, moved to tears by her extraordinary faith, courage and the unjust way she has been treated by Church authorities.

The following morning I went to the Ulster television studio for the recording. 'I am a priest,' I answered to one of the questions from interviewer Pat Coyle. At that stage, what else could I say? I wasn't being defiant. It's just I couldn't deny it.

That was the last interview I gave in connection with the conference. By the time I got home I was burnt out. I couldn't bear the least noise or stimulation. All I wanted was complete rest and silence. I went to the house of a friend who let me stay in bed for three days.

I had experienced the oppressive violence of the patriarchal institutional Church . That our conference happened at all, and had even been such a wonderful event, was a kind of a miracle. It happened despite the efforts of those who wanted to keep us invisible and silenced.

ಶ ಶ ಶ

ON A VISIT TO ASSISI, COLM AND I discovered a special fresco on a wall of the refectory of St Damiano monastery, where St Clare and her sisters had lived. The fresco depicts St Clare blessing the bread at the behest of the pope. It represents vividly the amazement of the pope and his cardinals as a ray of light (the Holy Spirit) comes through a window and crosses appear on the bread rolls as St Clare blesses them.

We had heard of this fresco, but it was not visible from the opening in the refectory, beyond which visitors were not allowed. Later we asked a Poor Clare sister why this magnificent fresco with its bright colours was kept hidden from visitors, and why they didn't have any reproductions for sale. Why keep it so hidden?

Her reply was, rather mysteriously, 'It is too early, it is not yet time'. To which Colm incredulously replied, 'After 800 years?'

St Clare of Assisi is often portrayed as sister moon to St Francis' sun, but she was no mere reflection; she radiated her own light. She was in truth a new leader of women. As I read more of her life story, I discovered that Clare too had to open up a path where there was none, and I found inspiration in her perseverance.

Clare discerned in herself a vocation, a way of following Christ, which didn't exist in the Church at the time. In fact, the door to any new calling was closed by the Lateran Council in 1215. Clare resisted the attempt to put all women religious under the Benedictine monastic rule, believing she was called to a radical form of poverty and would not settle for anything else.

She declared boldly, 'Holy Father, you can absolve me of my sins but I do not want you to absolve me of following Jesus Christ, my Lord'.

She became the first woman to write the rule of life for her order, the Order of the Poor Ladies. The pope finally approved it two days before she died in 1253. She had always known, better than the pope, about her true vocation, something I could relate to.

ಬ ಬ ಬ

WHILE THE DOOR TO ORDINATION WAS closed with *Ordinatio Sacerdatolis*, it did not stop Catholic women from being ordained. It just meant other ways were being found.

The first such woman I encountered in Ireland was Sister Frances Meigh, an iconographer. She came over from England and was ordained by Bishop Pat Buckley, himself a Catholic priest in Larne who had received apostolic succession from an independent bishop no longer in communion with Rome.

I went up to Larne to meet with Sister Frances on the eve of her ordination and wished her well on her path. I had no doubt, however, that it wasn't mine. Bishop Buckley did not ordain any other woman before his death in 2024.

I sought ordination from Auxiliary Bishop of Dublin Dermot O'Mahony who, as mentioned earlier, had been open and supportive. But in the end he declined. It wasn't to be.

But after the WOW International Conference in Dublin, the efforts to find ways for women to break the deadlock on ordination redoubled. Plans initiated by Austrian Christine Mayr-Lumetzberger led to her ordination as well as six other women by three independent Catholic bishops on 29 June 2002. I had been asked whether I wanted to join the Danube Seven, but again it didn't resonate with me so I declined.

After some of these women in turn became bishops a path was opened with the Association of Roman Catholic Women Priests now having a few hundred women ordained mostly, but not exclusively, in North America. I have met many of these women priests and bishops and several are frequent visitors, including Bishop Brigid Mary Meehan who was born in Ireland. But in all these years, I haven't found myself called to travel that route, to take that step.

I have been asked frequently, 'Have you been ordained?' And my answer has always been, 'No bishop has ever laid hands on me!'

It is not the fear of excommunication which keeps me from such ordination, but a deep sense that it is not in tune with my sense of calling. In many ways I know myself as a priest, with a sense that I have received the Sacrament of Orders through desire, just as one can receive a baptism of desire. In response to God's call, I said my yes, my 'fiat': 'Let it be done unto me according to your Word.'

'God has never given me a desire that He hasn't fulfilled,' said St Thérèse of Lisieux. If that desire is truly God's desire in me, God has already fulfilled it. Whether a bishop, or others, ever have the joy of laying hands on me remains an open question, even if the door still appears shut. Who knows what the future holds?

ഇ ഇ ഇ

THERE ARE DIFFERENT WAYS OF KNOWING. Of course, I knew that churchmen sometimes told lies, but it was rather theoretical. It wasn't until I heard a high ranking cleric lying in public that it truly registered with me.

I was in Rome in October 2001 at a shadow synod organised by Reform movements. The Synod of the People of God, as it was called, ended its deliberations with a petition to be handed in to Cardinal Schotte, who was secretary to the synod of bishops. The Dutch cardinal at first refused to receive our delegation, but as we made ourselves visibly noisy on the pavement outside his residence, the police prevailed upon him to open his door. A few of us were let in and handed in the petition.

Later on Cardinal Schotte was giving a press conference during which he was asked by a journalist: 'What do you think of the petition by the Synod of the People of God?'

'Never heard of them. Next question?'

I was shocked. It was such a bare-faced lie. I thought: If he lies about this, a relatively small issue, what else is he lying about? Lying seemed to be the easy way not to have to deal with uncomfortable issues. That day a lot of my trust crumbled.

After that I had no difficulty believing the reports of cover up of clerical sexual abuse which emerged, wave after wave, in Ireland and elsewhere. So many lies were exposed, revealing a culture of mendacity. Just like a cliff doesn't crumble with the power of just one wave but is slowly eroded with repeated waves, my trust in Church leaders slowly diminished until I found I had none left.

Too many betrayals, too many lies, too many mental reservations, too many deceptions, too many denials, too many failures to come clean and take responsibility. I had seen my trust abused too many times. It was like a well which had run bone dry. I remember praying before the Blessed Sacrament in St Thérèse Church when I realised that I have no trust left. I don't trust any of them, and that includes the pope, then Benedict XVI.

Churchmen had truly squandered the trust we had placed in them in order to preserve their powerful positions. Now that was gone. I once read about an American cardinal who had said, indignantly: 'I only lie when I have to!'

I came to the conclusion that they lied because they could. They could do it with impunity in a system where there is no accountability. Trust which had been freely given from now on would have to be earned. It made for a very different relationship.

On behalf of WOW we had organised for a banner to be displayed for a month from 4 October in Rome, calling for the ordination of women in several languages, including Latin! On October 6, twenty-five of us, wearing purple stoles, walked to where the banner was for a blessing ceremony. We were in the midst of our prayer service, with the banner hanging high above us, when we were interrupted by the Italian police. Three Carabinieri pointed at the banner six meters high above our heads: 'How did that get up there? Take it down presto! Show your identity papers!'

Although well outside the Vatican State, the banner was visible from windows in a corner of the Vatican, causing the ire of some monsignor who had called the police to have the offending object removed from his sight forthwith!

Fortunately for us, we had obtained a permit from the municipality of Rome and had paid for the banner to be displayed for a whole month.

The Carabinieri carefully examined our passports and the documents for the banner, questioning how we had got permission. Obviously it caused them much annoyance. They insisted they needed to see additional confirmation that this was legal. We were now worried they'd confiscate our passports. In desperation, someone contacted the man who had made the banner who came to pacify the police enough for them to leave us to resume our singing.

Between this and Cardinal Schotte, it was no wonder that by the time I got home to Dublin I was suffering from acute Vaticanitis. I have never been back. But our banner was lovely and as for the Vatican monsignor, he only had to look a it for a month outside his male fortress window.

∞ ∞ ∞

WHEN I STARTED CAMPAIGNING FOR the ordination of women the revelations of the clerical sexual abuse of children were still in the future. Like many others, I had been kept in the dark concerning the criminal actions of clerics. This was soon to change as courageous survivors managed to break through the omertà. Ireland was one of the first countries after the USA to start tackling that terrible scourge.

In the mid-1990s I joined a small prayer and reflection group including priests, religious and lay. One of these was a priest of Dublin diocese, Father Noel Reynolds. Noel had been a member of the Dublin Council of Priests and had sat on the sub-committee on Women in the Church. He was now parish priest of Glendalough, and we sometimes met in the parish house there. He seemed a gentle, quiet man.

In the late 1990s, Noel Reynolds was appointed as chaplain to the Rehabilitation Hospital in Dun Laoghaire and then retired for health reasons to a nursing home of the Little Sisters of the Poor in Roebuck. In 2001, Eamonn McCarthy and I invited him to lunch. As we were sitting down perusing the menu Noel Reynolds announced he had something to tell us. He said he was under garda investigation for having abused two girls, after the mother had complained, and wasn't denying the claims.

We were in complete shock: We had no inkling of it. If Noel hadn't told us we would have found it hard to believe. As it was, it was still difficult to get our heads around it. In April 2002 we heard Noel had died. I was still reeling with the shock of his revelation of abuse, but decided to go to his funeral. The Little Sisters of the Poor's chapel was packed with people. I wondered as I looked around: 'Who here knows about the abuse?'

As the funeral liturgy progressed I felt increasingly ill at ease. I couldn't believe my ears when I heard the choice of Gospel, 'Let the little children come onto me', and then a homily praising Noel for his pastoral ministry, including with children. Listening to all this, I kept thinking of the victims: How would they feel hearing this? I went home profoundly disturbed: 'I have taken part in a cover up.' I regretted attending a liturgy which, to me, lacked integrity and left a sour taste in my mouth.

In keeping with the funeral, Noel Reynolds was given a glowing obituary in the diocesan magazine. Soon after we learnt there had been complaints since 1995 and that he had abused around a hundred children. He is one of the priests named in the 2010 Murphy Report.

Over the decades I have read hundreds of testimonies of victims/survivors in Ireland and around the world. I have met and listened to several personally. I have watched several films in the cinema and online. I have read all the Irish official reports since the 2005 Ferns Report. I realise I was lucky never to be abused sexually, but that so many others weren't so fortunate and have paid a terrible price.

Above all, what they expose is something very dark, evil, in the Church, for there was a systemic dimension to it, to the crimes and the coverups. When the horrific revelations started coming thick and fast, I was confronted with how to respond. I decided I would not leave the Church but do all in my power, albeit limited, to help the victims/survivors get justice, heal wounds, and dismantle the architecture of coverup of criminality.

When the Independent Commission on Sexual Abuse in the Catholic Church (CIASE) in France report was released in October 2021, I watched the live presentation online. At the same time as I was listening to the harrowing testimonies from my home country, I received the first photos of our newborn grandson, born the day before on the feast of St Francis, and I wept yet again for the betrayal of innocence in so many children. 'What you do to the least of my brothers and sisters you do it to me.' Do we really believe it?

ಜಾ ಜಾ ಜಾ

Every year I have celebrated the anniversary of my baptism. In 2002 I was inspired to mark it in a special way by going to St Brigid's Well in Kildare, and asked Eamonn McCarthy to come with me.

I had been at the Well several times before to absorb its peaceful feminine energy and to connect with St Brigid. But now I wanted to do something which expressed what had been with me over the summer. I had a purple stole, the symbol of women waiting for ordination, which had been given to me by the German group Lila Stole and which I had worn on many occasions.

In the brilliant sunshine, I blessed myself with the cool water from the Well, remembering my baptism. I contemplated the statue of St Brigid holding her torch aloft, and then I hung my purple stole on a branch of a tree nearby. It was time for me to let go of that symbol of waiting. I said a prayer to St Brigid, asking for her help, and left the purple stole fluttering in the breeze, like a proud banner.

In August 2018, during the World Meeting of Families, I was back at the same Well with delegates from Women's Ordination Worldwide for a prayer service, under the watchful eye of St Brigid. And on the anniversary of my baptism, we celebrated Eucharist together.

☙ ☙ ☙

THE IMMIGRATION OFFICER AT Melbourne Airport couldn't believe his ears: 'You are going on to Hobart for an international conference on the ordination of women? Well, good luck to you!' He laughed, not unkindly, as he handed me back my passport.

I could understand his amusement; to some extent I shared it too. I had never dreamt my sense of vocation would bring me 'down under', and to Tasmania to boot, but I was delighted to attend a well organised event by Ordination of Catholic Women (OCW) with one hundred participants from around the globe. I was given the honour to open the conference which had for theme, 'Shaping Change, Women, the Diaconate and Priestly Ordination in the Roman Catholic Church'. It was a follow up to the WOW Dublin Conference the previous year.

My speech contained a simple message: 'Do not wait any longer. Now is the time.' And, I added, speaking from experience: 'As long as we are prepared to wait, we shall be kept waiting. And if we are prepared to wait for ever, well we shall indeed be kept waiting for ever.'

I went on, taking as a model of faith Mary of Nazareth who, at the Annunciation, said Yes to God without waiting for permission from any external source, be it husband or religious authority. If she had, I added, she would have been told it was impossible and we would still be waiting for Jesus to be born! And of course since we were in Australia, I mentioned the testimony of Australian Sister Irene McCormack, martyred in Peru:

> Not only is it a contradiction to the proclamation of Jesus that there is no distinction between male and female, but a lack of appreciation of the plight of villagers like ours all over the world, that our Church continues denying its official ministry, that is by nature communion.

I concluded by repeating my message, with urgency:

> Let us not wait to open ourselves and our communities to the power of the Holy Spirit, under the pretext that we cannot do so without permission.

I spelt it out clearly:

> If women were only saying No to the religious authorities, they would be mere rebels and it would be only acts of defiance, annoying but stoppable. But women who say Yes to God are unstoppable.

Obviously that distinction was too subtle for the local newspaper. The following morning there was a large photo of me in *The Mercury* with the headline: 'Rebel in Fight for Women Priests.'

Colm and I went on to Sydney for a few days, meeting more people, and doing radio and television interviews. I flew to Canberra to be on Paul Collins religious show on ABC Television. I returned home to Ireland early December, jet-lagged but happy to have helped break the deadly silence imposed on us. I was relieved, too, to be back in time to be at the bedside of Colm's mother, Rosheen, as she died on 19 December.

႙   ႙   ႙

IN JANUARY 2003, EAMONN MCCARTHY arranged for me to meet informally with Bishop Eamonn Walsh, who was an auxiliary bishop in Dublin and administrator for the diocese of Ferns. I was able to share with him some of my spiritual journey and sense of vocation. Bishop Walsh listened attentively. As we were leaving he expressed regret that God hadn't made it more clear if He really wanted women priests, to which I replied it would never be clear enough for some.

But then he went on to say as we parted, 'Perhaps one of your sons will have your vocation'. I was speechless. That statement burrowed into my heart. If it is my vocation, why can I not live it? Why does it take a male to be able to live it out? Surely it made no sense.

As a parent I was well aware of the danger of projecting one's own unfulfilled desires onto our children. I certainly didn't want one of my sons to live out *my* vocation. If God called me, it's me God wants. And what would Bishop Walsh have said if I had no children, or only daughters? What would happen to my vocation? The fact that he had said 'your vocation' made me think that at one level he recognised a genuine calling in me, but could only imagine a 'solution' that kept the patriarchal exclusion intact.

The following days I found I couldn't get his parting comment out of my mind. Eventually, I decided I would write to him to express how wounding I had found his statement. He replied, offering to meet again to clear the air. Appropriately, we met in a café called Encore!

I explained why his suggestion about my vocation going to my son not only made no sense to me but was deeply hurtful. He answered he had offered it to me as a way of comforting me, thinking it would make me feel better, similar to what he said to men who had to leave the priesthood to get married. At least we were able to have a very frank sharing. I left with a measure of peace, glad I had said what I needed to say, and grateful he had made himself vulnerable enough to hear it.

8.

Mary of Magdala

I knew there would be opposition from people, besides the Church hierarchy, but I couldn't have anticipated the myriad forms it would take. Perhaps being a woman with a foreign-sounding name made me a target for a lot of negativity. A few examples:

When we were collecting petitions in Grafton Street, some American tourists accused us of being communists, which baffled us until we realised for them that's the worst insult imaginable.

There were plenty of ad hominem insults too, mocking my appearance: The most memorable is the person who loudly made fun of what she called my 'rabbit teeth'.

The biggest sacrifice was the loss of my privacy and anonymity. I soon realised why others didn't want to go public and expose themselves to ridicule, insults and threats.

Taking part in radio interviews could be very challenging, especially when people phoned in. Early on I appeared on a program with Pat Kenny, then on RTÉ 1, and left in tears. I told Eamonn: 'You could discern your vocation quietly and have it tested in the seminary, why do I have to expose myself to the whole nation?'

Everybody felt free to analyse me and to express their opinions on air, a popular one dismissing me as 'that woman going through a midlife crisis, she is an attention-seeker'.

Or, as one Kerry priest vehemently insisted, 'She is not even Irish, she is importing these ideas from pagan France.' I could reply I was as Irish as St Patrick and an Irish citizen as well, but obviously not Irish enough. Some even wrote that they would pay for me and my family to go back to where I came from!

If it was painful to hear, at least there was a degree of moderation on radio shows. There was no such filter on the anonymous phone calls and letters which followed my interviews. Almost all of these used sexual language, calling me 'a whore, a scarlet woman'. The letters were often signed, 'A good Christian'. Some of the phone calls were vicious, men threatening me with 'violence and rape to put me right'.

On one occasion, I had just put down the phone after such a tirade when our son Killian, seeing the tears in my eyes, asked, 'Why are you crying?' What could I answer? Tell my innocent child that I had been threatened in the foulest words with gang rape?

Such calls could come in at any time of the day or night. It became so bad I eventually made the decision to go ex-directory, to remove my name from the phone book. I was reluctant to do so as it felt like a defeat, but it was a necessary step. Later on the issue became abusive emails. The ones with violent pornographic content I reported to the Gardaí.

I hadn't expected the insults and threats of rape, but speaking with a woman back in France who also went public with her vocation to the priesthood I realised it was a common reaction. A woman voicing her calling to the priesthood brought up the worst misogynistic violence in some men.

It certainly challenged some clerics at a visceral level. I was taken aback when once, outside the church after a funeral, a priest I didn't know came up to me and shouted in my face: 'Women priests? Over my dead body!' I wondered whether he would have hit me if we weren't surrounded by people.

There were many more who chose to respond with mockery and ridicule. I got used to being referred to as 'that wannabe priest'. A French priest I knew who was sent as a nuncio to an African country took the trouble to write to me: 'Thank God, there are no would-be priestesses here!'

As the years passed by, there was plenty of taunting, 'Are you not ordained yet?' And on and on it went. As recently as last year, after a family funeral, the priest had to vent his feelings: 'You're not ordained yet? You're waiting to be made a bishop?'

Maybe the most bizarre incident was when I met an older priest I knew in a supermarket. He launched into a tirade at the top of his voice, as bemused shoppers wondered what this was all about: 'It's your fault there are no vocations to the priesthood! It's because of you that Clonliffe had to close!' (The Dublin seminary in Clonliffe had closed in 2001, despite a last ditch effort with a 'men in black' advertising campaign.) As he went on holding me responsible for the crisis, I had to wonder at the degree of power he was attributing to me. I was another Eve who deserved to be blamed for the fall, this time for the fall in male celibate vocations to the priesthood. It was both funny and tragic.

A Divine Calling

ಙ ಙ ಙ

I HAD BEEN DRAWN TO THE MINISTRY of spiritual guidance for many years. Some people had been coming to me informally, so I felt the time had come to train formally.

After a few enquiries I applied to the Jesuits in Manresa House in Clontarf, who were offering a two year course in spiritual direction. I wasn't confident of being accepted because of my identification with women priests, but in due course I was called for an interview. The interview with one Jesuit was quite searching, as it had to be. For whatever reason, I only remember one question: 'What was my favourite spiritual text?'

I replied, the 'Song of Songs'. He then asked me what commentary on the 'Song of Songs' I liked best, and I replied, 'The one the Holy Spirit is writing in my heart'. I could tell by his silent pause it wasn't what he expected. I left wondering whether I had blown my chances, but no, I was accepted.

I arrived for the first weekend in September and felt at ease meeting the other participants in our group of about a dozen people. A Jesuit and a religious sister were running the course. Everything went well, and on Saturday night I reflected on how happy I was to have embarked on the course, how I felt at home.

On Sunday morning we had some spiritual exercises and then a short break before Mass. I took the opportunity to get some fresh air in the grounds, and while walking a prayer rose within me: 'Give me a heart that can refuse you nothing'. The answer came, 'I already have'. I was left baffled as to what had prompted me to ask this in prayer, at this moment. It would soon be made clear.

As I came back to the room where Mass was to be celebrated I realised an issue had surfaced in my absence and one person was quite distressed. That person, who belonged to the Church of Ireland, had asked in advance, and had been refused, permission to receive Communion. I was shocked, but there was no time to discuss it, as Mass was starting. We were sitting in a small circle and I sat on the person's left. I wondered, what should I do?

The time for Communion came, the priest received first and then the paten with a carefully counted number of hosts (minus one) was passed around as each said 'the Body of Christ' and 'Amen'. When the Church of Ireland person's turn came they said 'Amen' but, as instructed, didn't take a host and passed the paten to me. In that instant I knew what to do: I refused to receive. I passed on the paten and the priest consumed the host I had left behind. When the cup was passed around, I also didn't partake. For me, the Body of Christ wasn't just the consecrated elements but ourselves, and the exclusion of that member contradicted that.

As the Mass ended, I was in disbelief at what I had witnessed. An hour beforehand I was happy to be in the course, now it had all crumbled. I wanted to raise the issue there and then, but there was no opportunity. I mentioned it to another Jesuit, whom I knew, who answered, 'What planet are you living on?' which only made me feel worse. After a quick lunch I could barely eat, I went home, wondering what to do next.

My participation on the course ended, 'died', during that Eucharist. I still hoped things could change, however it was made clear to me the rule would remain. I realised there was no way I could participate with integrity in the Eucharist month after month while that person would be excluded. It went against everything I had come to believe deep in my heart about my faith. And my trust in the course had completely shattered.

I asked for a meeting with the Jesuit director of Manresa, but the gulf in understanding between us was apparent. For me, the exclusion of that person was as scandalous as if a mother refused to feed one of her children around the table. For the Jesuit, that rule was made by the pastors in Rome, 'and the pastors know best'. At which point I replied that surely we now knew that 'the pastors know best' wasn't true, given the revelations of clerical child sexual abuses and cover-ups. What need for discernment if all we need is a rule book?

I eventually had to face reality and make the decision to leave the course. It was very painful. I so wanted to train as a spiritual director, but deep down I knew I couldn't compromise my integrity. I was grieving and bewildered. How to understand God's will in all this?

That short inner prayer dialogue before that fateful Eucharistic celebration remained my guiding light in the darkness I was now in: 'Give me a heart that can refuse You nothing' and the response of 'I have'. I understood that I had to sacrifice my participation on the course.

Everybody had to make their own decision. The person who was refused Communion decided to stay on the course but thanked me for my support. But I couldn't stay. I dearly wished I could, but I wouldn't have been able to look at myself in the mirror. It would have amounted to a total betrayal. I asked for and got a refund of my course fee, on the basis that it was wrongly described as an Ecumenical course but wasn't in practice.

To all intents and purposes my hope of training as a spiritual director had died. It looked like I had killed it by my inability to comply with the rules. Yet again I asked myself why couldn't I just accept what everybody else seemed able to do, why I couldn't just fit in? Was there anywhere for me?

Months later, when I mentioned to Sister Bernadette Flanagan what had happened, she informed me that a new course was about to start that might be suitable for me. The course was being run by two lay women, Geraldine Holton and Carmel Boyle, in the An Croí centre, then in Ashbourne, County Meath. I applied and was accepted after an interview in 2004 and did the two year training.

It was not always easy and there were teething problems as we were the first intake for this new course, but it provided a solid formation, and was up to date and innovative in both breadth and depth. There was a great variety of inputs, with lecturers from different backgrounds, including from abroad. I was able to focus on the Carmelite mystical tradition. I also made deep and lasting friendships.

I am immensely grateful to the course organisers who had the vision, courage and enterprising spirit to set it up. In 2006 I graduated with a Pontifical Diploma in Spiritual Direction in a ceremony in Milltown.

I was accredited by the All Ireland Spiritual Guides Association (AISGA) and have been practicing ever since as a spiritual director, accompanying people between the ages of 20 and 80, women and men, lay, religious, priests, missionaries, students, each on a unique spiritual journey.

I can only say that it has been deeply fulfilling to be able to minister in that way and to witness how the Spirit in each person grows ever stronger.

ಬಿ ಬಿ ಬಿ

I HAD WRITTEN TO THE NEW ARCHBISHOP of Dublin, Diarmuid Martin, asking for a meeting, but hadn't got a reply. Some people I knew who had written to him about diverse issues also hadn't got replies, so it wasn't promising.

When in Rwanda in June 2004, the last thing my missionary friend Geneviève told me at the airport was: 'Do ask again for that meeting with Diarmuid Martin, it's important.' So I promised I would, and wrote again on my return to Dublin, but to no avail.

On the morning of my birthday, I woke up with an inner question: 'What do you want for your birthday?' Immediately my response came: 'A meeting with the archbishop!' And then the inner reply: 'Pick up the telephone and ask for a meeting.'

As it was still too early to phone Archbishop's House, I turned on the radio to listen to the news. Imagine my surprise on hearing that another letter of mine was published in *The Irish Times* and read on 'What's in the Papers' on RTÉ Radio1. Now that was a first!

Vatican View of Women

(Letters to the editor, The Irish Times, 4 August 2004)

Madam,

The latest Vatican document on women (IT, August 2nd) lists 'listening, welcoming, humility, faithfulness, praise and waiting' as essential aspects of

Christian life and goes on to say that 'women in fact live them with particular intensity and naturalness'.

I can only conclude that it is these very qualities which, in the eyes of the Vatican, make us unfit for the ordained ministries.

Yours, Soline Vatinel

I still had a smile on my face when I phoned Archbishop's House. The secretary who answered told me the archbishop was away until September. Did I want to see somebody else? I said no, it was personal. I had waited long enough, I could wait a little longer.

And lo and behold I finally did get a letter offering me a meeting on 1 October. I was delighted it was on the feast of St Thérèse, but it would be during my teaching time in Sion Hill so I had to ask for another date. I feared I might have to wait a long time, but was actually offered an earlier date, 23 September.

When the day came, Colm drove me and waited in the car. It was the first time I was back in Archbishop's House since my meeting with Cardinal Desmond Connell in 1994. A lot had happened for me since. This time we were in a larger room and sitting further apart.

I told Diarmuid Martin I wanted him to hear first hand, not just from media reports, about my sense of vocation to the priesthood and why I was doing what I was doing. I also wanted him to know how Eamonn McCarthy, a priest of the diocese whom he had known in seminary, had come to support women's ordination, for which he had been sidelined.

So I shared some of my personal spiritual journey with the archbishop, and to his credit he listened, which was more than his predecessor had done. But I could sense it was hard for him to hear what I was describing, and there certainly was no encouragement to continue. I had to make myself share what I wanted to share, aware of his resistance to it.

'Had he met before other women with a calling to priesthood?' I asked.

'Yes, Anglican women.'

'But no Catholic woman?'

'No'

He reminded me of what John Paul II had declared in *Ordinatio Sacerdatolis* about reserving the priesthood to men alone, who alone could represent Christ.

I said we had a great theology of creation about the equality of men and women made in the image of God, but *Ordinatio Sacerdatolis* was undermining it, and also our theology of incarnation and redemption, since only what Christ has assumed has been redeemed.

If Christ's incarnation is limited to maleness, women are not redeemed. Furthermore, I said, how is it that the women disciples received directly the Holy Spirit at Pentecost, but now can only do so through men? He offered no response to these theological questions.

I told him how I had come to start presiding at Eucharist (which had become public knowledge). I wanted him to hear from me what was behind the headlines. I wasn't seeking his permission, or his endorsement, or even his understanding. What I wanted was for me to be able to tell him face to face.

He replied, 'Now, if every seminarian who is not accepted for ordination went home and celebrated Eucharist, where would we be?'

'I am sorry, but this is not my case. There has never been a discernment process. My sense of vocation has been rejected just because I am a woman.'

The meeting was drawing to a close as he had to be somewhere else. As we were standing he told me, 'This is not a threat, but it is my duty to warn you that you are risking excommunication'.

To which I replied: 'I am well aware of it, and it's not a risk I take lightly, but I must follow my conscience.'

There followed a brief exchange on the treatment of prophets. We were both aware of the gravity of my situation. As we were now standing on the porch I interjected a light note: 'Today is the feast day of Padre Pio who got me this appointment with you!' I said with a smile.

The archbishop, surprised, smiled back: 'I didn't know you were a devotee.'

'I need all the help I can get!'

That was probably the one thing we could both agree on. I left him with a handshake (no kiss this time!).

I was at peace. I had spoken what was in my heart, he had listened and said what he felt he had to say. It had been a respectful exchange. In the course of our meeting Archbishop Martin had asked me whether I had put in writing what I was sharing with him about my sense of vocation. So the following day I sent him a copy of my talk at the 1995 BASIC seminar and the more recent spiritual autobiography I had written for my An Croí course in Spiritual direction. I felt then I had discharged my responsibility towards him.

A week later, on 30 September, the archbishop phoned Eamonn McCarthy and offered him an appointment as curate in Donard and Davidstown, County Wicklow, after five years in the wilderness – a gift for Eamonn on his birthday!

ஐ   ஐ   ஐ

I HAVE HAD SEVERAL SIGNIFICANT DREAMS over the years, but one remains clear in my memory. I had been consumed with the desire to meet with Pope John Paul II for a long time and made several attempts to do so, with no success.

One night I actually dreamt that I was at a meeting with him. In the dream I heard myself tell him about my sense of calling to the presbyteral ministry. He started getting angry, but then remembered he had told me to speak freely, and motioned me to go on. Then, when I had finished, he said: 'I must arrange for you to meet with somebody higher up.' I was dumbfounded. I thought: 'He is the pope. At the summit of the hierarchical pyramid. Who is higher? God?' I couldn't fathom who he meant. But he then went on: 'You must meet with Cardinal Joseph Ratzinger'. With these words I woke up.

The dream was so impressed on my mind that after some time I decided I would indeed write to Cardinal Joseph Ratzinger at the Congregation for the Doctrine of the Faith. I got no reply.

A few years later, John Paul II died on 2 April 2005. After such a long pontificate, 27 years, which covered all my adult years, there was a sense of hope for some of us that there may be, at last, an opening to change. Like many people around the world I watched news of the conclave and waited to hear who was the new pope when the white smoke went up. A very familiar name: Joseph Ratzinger! I knew then it would be more of the same, no opening, perhaps even worse.

On the screen we could see jubilant crowds in St Peter Square. I didn't share in that jubilation. The phone started ringing. Friends were devastated, many said they couldn't endure any more, they had been hanging in by their fingernails, but now that was the end. What about me?

On three different occasions that week, I had heard these words of Scripture: 'Trust in God still and trust in me' (John 14:1). Now, in the midst of my deep disappointment, they anchored me, and called out to not give up. But there was no denying that the election of Pope Benedict XVI, as Joseph Ratzinger called himself, was a blow. It felt a bit like a prison sentence had been extended. The wintry years would continue.

༄ ༄ ༄

WHEN IN MARCH 2006 COLM TOLD ME that Mick Peelo of RTÉ had phoned about doing a programme, a *Would You Believe?* special, incorporating the filming of me presiding at a Eucharist, I initially didn't welcome the idea. In fact, I found myself filled with fear at the prospect. I thought of running off, leaving the island, taking the ferry to France – escaping just like Jonah. But I resisted and agreed to hear what they had in mind. I was adamant that I would not do anything that didn't feel right and that I wouldn't let RTÉ impose an agenda.

A Divine Calling

I had a long chat with Mick Peelo and he persuaded me. I sensed that it was indeed a God-given opportunity. In the course of our conversation Mick spotted our painting of Mary of Magdala preaching and inquired about her. I explained that she is the apostle to the apostles, first witness to the Risen Christ, and that there is a sanctuary dedicated to her in the South of France. I had been there with Colm in 2003, after which we had commissioned the painting from Emer O'Boyle. It was a very different story to the distorted image of her as a penitent sinner associated with the Magdalen laundries.

RTÉ decided we would go to her shrine in La Sainte Baume, between Nice and Marseilles. We arrived on Ascension Thursday, very appropriately as the Risen Christ entrusts Mary Magdalen with the news of his forthcoming ascension. The RTÉ team of three men couldn't have been better, very friendly and professional. I was completely at ease with them.

While there was plenty of filming, it was also for me a real pilgrimage, with times of solitude and silence. We spent time in the impressive old basilica dedicated to the saint in the town. Then I stayed on my own overnight in the pilgrim's hostel and the following day we climbed up in the Mediterranean heat to the cave where the shrine is. I took part in the Mass there, and afterwards had a good exchange with the Dominican friar in charge while RTÉ filmed.

After that there was a long interview filmed in the forest below, where I recounted the difficult vocational path I had travelled so far. It was appropriate this was taking place in my home country of origin, where my faith journey had started and been nurtured. And of course one of my middle names is Madeleine.

Back in Dublin the thought came to me that if RTÉ were to film a celebration of the Eucharist, it should definitely be on the Feast of Pentecost. As it happens, that was the date they had actually scheduled for a technical reason!

So a group of us gathered around a table in our sun-filled kitchen. There were men and women of different ages, some had come from as far as Antrim. All were conscious they were bearing witness to a reality they believed in, as they were taking the courageous step to be present and be filmed.

I was wondering whether I would find it distracting, but it didn't interfere at all with my praying. It was a joy-filled celebration, bathed in sunlight. In the middle of the table draped in red for Pentecost was a large candle I had brought back from La Sainte Baume.

At the end of the filming I had a great sense of 'mission accomplished'. I was glad I hadn't yielded to my initial fear and declined. I joked with the RTÉ producer: 'Well it looks like neither of us are in charge!'

After that, there was the long wait for it to be shown. I didn't know what the edited result would look like, how it would be woven with the interviews of the other participants, one of whom was the renowned theologian Mary T. Malone, author of *Women in Christianity*, *The Elephant in the Church* and *Praying with the Women Mystics*.

It was broadcast on a dark evening at the end of November, but the programme was filled with light. It was the second part of a programme on the priesthood, 'Last Judgement', the first part a week earlier had dealt with the issue of celibacy. As I watched the programme in which I appeared under the name 'Soline Humbert', having taken on my mother's name the year before, I thought RTÉ had done an excellent job, respectful and true to what I had shared.

The programme had barely ended when the phone rang. Michael Keane, a Mayo priest and a good friend, was bursting with delight and congratulations. After that the phone never stopped for the rest of the night with friends expressing their support. One call did surprise me, however, coming from a quite conservative couple we knew from the Teams of Our Lady. No, they weren't shocked, in fact they were pleased and wanted to let me know.

A few days later I was going into Dublin on the train when I saw an older woman observing me. 'Did I see you on television the other night?'

'Yes, you did,' I replied, not quite sure what her reaction would be.

'You were very good. About time we have women priests!'

I couldn't but reflect on how times had changed. The sky hadn't fallen because a married Catholic woman had presided at Eucharist and the people weren't in shock.

I went to a bookshop where the Passionist priest, Brian d'Arcy, was doing a signing. He caught sight of me and exclaimed, with a smile, in a loud voice for all to hear: 'There's the woman who celebrates Mass in her kitchen!' Heads turned around and I smiled back.

ಲ ಲ ಲ

MY FRIEND DELMA SHERIDAN INTRODUCED me to the Ecumenical Conference which took place in the Benedictine Abbey of Glenstal every year in June. I accompanied her for several summers and always looked forward to it.

There was much to nourish the mind and the spirit, with enriching conversations with diverse participants. One experience has remained vividly with me.

As a member of Spiritual Directors International, I receive the quarterly journal *Presence*. As I opened it, I was taken by an article by Ekman Tam entitled, 'The Road to Emmaus: A Biblical Rationale for Spiritual Direction'. I was familiar already with the passage (Luke 24:13-35) but it somehow held me very strongly.

The following day, at breakfast, one of the organisers asked me whether I would agree to do one of the readings during the morning prayer service. After I agreed I was astonished when he told me it was the Gospel's account on the road to Emmaus!

When the time came I went up and started reading. I was a few lines into the text when I felt something inside me, a presence, as I read on. At the same time I became aware of a great stillness in the chapel. When I had finished and walked back to my seat, I could see some people were in tears.

After the service ended, several people told me how moved they had been by my reading, that I had read 'beautifully'. I knew they were referring to that mysterious Presence I had felt. To me, it was the Risen Christ made present through the Word.

A few weeks after the conference I was contacted by a fellow participant. 'I have been thinking of you and Mary of Magdala a lot and I have come to Dublin to give you something.' I was intrigued. Much to my surprise he handed me a small black leather case. I took out a little round metal container.

'It's for holy oils,' he explained.

As I slipped the holding ring onto my thumb he went on: 'Sorry, they are designed for a big male thumb, but it's for you, to do the anointing of the sick.' I was completely speechless.

'Do you not like it?'

'No, it's just I am very moved, I don't know what to say; just thank you.'

ଓ ଓ ଓ

ON COMPLETION OF MY TRAINING as a spiritual director I started looking for employment in ministry. In May 2007 I saw an ad for a post of pastoral worker in Rathgar parish and decided to apply. I was familiar with the area, as I had lived around there in my early years in college.

I was called for an interview before three people, two women and the parish priest, and answered all their questions. I was pleased to be appointed, on 22 July, the feast of Mary of Magdala. I then had a meeting with the parish priest who showed me my office in the Church of the Three Patrons and drove me around the parish. I was due to start on 8 September. In the meantime, as having a car was a requirement for the job, I went out and bought one. I named it Assumpta, in honour of the feast and on the assumption I had a job.

A week later, on 22 August, a letter from the Parish priest landed through the letter box. I wondered why is he writing to me? The answer was in the first line: 'I regret to inform you I must withdraw the offer of employment because of your issues with the archbishop.' It continued with offering the possibility of a meeting if that would be helpful to me.

It was like a bolt from the blue and I felt sick. My job had just crumbled. I decided I did indeed need a meeting. I knew the termination was final, so it wasn't in the hope of reviving the job, but I owed it to myself to have a face to face meeting.

I drove there in my little brand new car, purchased specially for a job which no longer existed. The parish priest and one of the women who had interviewed me were there. I had been particularly incensed by the reference in the letter to 'your issues with the archbishop', without specifying what those were.

I started by saying: 'I want to put it on record that I have never abused sexually a child or anybody else.'

They immediately apologised, 'No, no, of course not, we never wanted to imply that.'

'Well then, what did you mean by my issues with the archbishop? Has Archbishop Diarmuid Martin said anything about my appointment? Has he objected?' I felt they were hiding behind the archbishop. They had to confess that he hadn't. He was spending August in Rome and my lowly appointment was not on his agenda.

They finally explained the real reason: 'We didn't know when we appointed you that you had celebrated the Eucharist.'

It was my turn to be shocked. How could they not have known? It had been so public on national television. Had none of them seen or heard of that *Would You Believe?* programme?

It wasn't credible, but that's what they said. They then went on to re-affirm that I was the best candidate for the job, that they supported my work for women's ordination and that they admired me. But they had decided I couldn't have the post. It was like rubbing salt in my wound. Were they trying to make themselves feel better?

I cut short the *plámos*: 'Don't admire me, imitate me.' There was nothing more to be said.

Later on I cried about the loss of the job. I realised it wasn't just that particular post, but that all employment in the institutional Church was now closed to me. I was outside the pale, an outlaw. I felt the pain very deeply. It was a deep wounding and it would take many months of shedding copious tears swimming in the Irish Sea.

At some stage I felt the need to re-visit the Church of the Three Patrons, where my office would have been. In the darkened church I prayed the Stations of the Cross. The Station where Jesus is stripped of his garments held me. I had been 'stripped' of that post. I then lit a candle but I didn't put my few cents in the coin box: I decided Rathgar parish owed me a small candle!

Some friends said I should sue the parish, but there was nothing to be gained going the legal route. I would have to shake the dust off my feet and continue my journey. I had several vivid dreams at that time, some of them contained violence, reflecting the spiritual trauma I felt, but I also had one of a bird in a cage. It helped me realise I would have lost my freedom and been caged in the Rathgar job. I was jobless and unemployable in the Church, but at least I was free.

I WENT BACK TO LOURDES A SECOND time, at the invitation of my friend Delma in the summer of 2008. We spent an enjoyable week, a mixture of spiritual retreat, pilgrimage in the morning, and in the afternoon time together visiting places.

The following day, 12 May, was our departure day with our flight in the evening. I had planned to have a late breakfast, pack my bags and vacate the hotel room as late as possible. But it was not to be.

For some reason I woke up at dawn. Everything was quiet, not a sound in the hotel or outside. I tried to go back to sleep but an inner voice told me to get up. I got dressed and tiptoed down the stairs as quietly as I could. At reception I hung up my room key at the board and was nearly out the door when the receptionist called to me: 'There is somebody who needs a priest.' He gave me a room number on the fourth floor.

I went up to the fourth floor and heard a woman's voice calling out softly, in English, 'Sacred Heart of Jesus, Sacred Heart of Jesus, Sacred Heart of Jesus.' I knocked at the bedroom door, which was slightly open, and inside I found a woman who had just discovered that her husband had died during the night. They were from Northern Ireland and were due to fly back that morning.

I introduced myself and offered my help, which she accepted. I said prayers with her and together we blessed the body with Lourdes water. I lit a candle. I told her I would deal with the doctor who agreed to release the body for the funeral undertakers in the afternoon. I said to her, 'I want you to know the Sacred Heart heard your prayer. You asked for a priest. He woke me up so that I could help.' As it happens, I had just bought a modern representation of the Sacred Heart which I had propped up in front of my bed (I never thought it would act as an early morning alarm clock!).

After she had gone I waked the dead man for the rest of the morning. In the afternoon I had a great desire to attend Mass and came across one intended for a group of Dutch pilgrims, so I joined in. I went back to the hotel just in time for the funeral team to collect the body of the deceased. As I shared the events of the day with Delma she agreed that it was an extraordinary ending to our pilgrimage.

Lourdes was full of priests, the hotel was full of priests, but I was the one who got called!

ಐ ಐ ಐ

EXCOMMUNICATION WASN'T SOMETHING I was familiar with until it became a sword of Damocles hanging over my head, and the heads of all others involved in the movement for women's ordination.

I had mistakenly thought excommunication was in the past, with people like Henry VIII, Galileo, Luther and heresy trials, but somehow the 1990s brought it back into fashion. The Curia brandished it as its favourite weapon to keep women in check, as well as any men who supported them.

Thankfully, I never considered excommunication as having the power to cut me off from God's love, which is all that matters to me. I wholeheartedly believe what St Paul affirms: 'Nothing can separate us from the love of God.' But I knew that for some, especially older women and men, it still carried a lot of weight due to the fear that they wouldn't be allowed a funeral Mass in church.

For others, religious sisters and priests especially, excommunication meant they would be expelled from their religious orders or priestly ministry. It may not have the power to separate them from the love of God, but it could result in a lot of psychological and financial hardship.

Tissa Balasurriya was excommunicated for supporting women priests in his book on Mary, until he withdrew some statements. Then Roy Bourgeois, a US priest, was excommunicated and expelled from the Maryknoll for his courageous support of women's ordination. And as we have seen, Sister Joan Chittister and Sister Myra Poole were threatened with it in an attempt to prevent them from attending the 2001 Dublin WOW Conference.

The first women ordained on the Danube in 2002 (the 'Danube Seven') were of course also formally excommunicated. And at least one English woman who attended women's ordinations in Canada also was formally excommunicated with severe consequences for her teaching job. In 2014, the head of We Are Church Austria and her husband, Martha and Gert Heizer, were also excommunicated for celebrating Mass without an ordained priest.

Seán Fagan, an Irish Marist priest and gifted moral theologian, was also threatened with excommunication for writing in favour of women's ordination in a letter to *The Irish Times* in 2008. The CDF demanded that the Marists force him to publicly recant and he was hounded by the CDF right up to his death in 2016, as related by Angela Hanley in her book *What happened to Fr Seán Fagan?*' Seán used to say to me, 'We will survive,' to which I would reply, 'We will do more than survive, we will flourish.' Those were dark days.

And while he has not been threatened with excommunication, Redemptorist priest Father Tony Flannery was suspended in 2012 from public ministry because of his support for women's ordination and changes in Church sexual teachings. He remains suspended to this day. He has written about the abusive CDF process in his book *A Question of Conscience*.

Several women have been ordained 'in the catacomb', meaning their identity hasn't been made public, to avoid excommunication. Women being ordained ('attempting to be ordained') are considered to have excommunicated themselves automatically, besides their ordination being deemed invalid. Women presiding at Eucharist ('attempting to') are in the same category of excommunication *latae sententiae*. As mentioned, Archbishop Diarmuid Martin warned me I was risking excommunication for doing just that.

Many people have asked me whether I have been excommunicated. To this day I have not received any formal notice that I am, and as for excommunication *latae sententiae*, I have never believed what I was doing was a 'grave crime', and so I have never considered myself excommunicated.

In April 2009 I attended a conference and celebration Mass for Mary Ward, foundress of the Institute of the Blessed Virgin Mary and, ironically, condemned and jailed as a 'heretic, rebel and schismatic' by the Inquisition, only to be praised centuries later by Pope Pius XII as 'that incomparable woman'.

In all the years I have never been refused Communion, for which I am grateful.

It seems to be easier to threaten to excommunicate women and men than to acknowledge there is an urgent issue with the exclusion of women from ministering the sacraments. And I would argue that it is better to be excommunicated for supporting women's ordination than committing sexual violence against children and/or covering up these crimes, which, incredibly, do not incur excommunication. This speaks volumes about the Church's values and priorities.

ཨོཾ ཨོཾ ཨོཾ

As I HAVE WRITTEN BEFORE, it is the saints who choose us. That's clearly the case for St John Vianney, for I would not have chosen him! He first entered my life in a 'holy picture' my religion teacher gave me as a memento for my Profession of Faith. On it there was a quote from him: 'Our sins are like grains of sands besides the mountain of God's mercy.'

In 1969, the new Roman calendar moved his feast day to the day of his death, 4 August, my birthday! It wasn't until 1990 that I developed a real connection with him, facilitated by the fact that my brother had moved to Lyon and John Vianney's village of Ars is in that region.

As a woman with a call to the priesthood who is facing big obstacles, I could relate to him who was initially rejected, considered unsuitable for the priesthood. Even after his ordination, for several years he was considered not competent enough to hear confessions. Later, he ended up being canonised as patron saint of parish priests, which proves God has a sense of humour!

His theology may not be exactly mine, for he was a man of his century, but I could resonate with the mystic with a big pastoral heart on a personal level. In 2008, I saw a poster advertising the celebrations in Ars for the 150th anniversary of his death the following year. Imagine my surprise when early in 2009 we got an invitation to attend my nephew's wedding early August, which meant that I could be in Ars on the special feast day. It felt like John Vianney himself wanted me there!

9.

No Woman, No Church

Many older people remember where they were when they heard President John Kennedy had been shot. Similarly, I remember where I was when I heard that Pope Benedict XVI had resigned on 11 February 2013. I was visiting a friend when she heard the news: a papal resignation, the first in 600 years! While others were stunned, angry or felt betrayed, I had a sense of something lifting.

So now there was another papal election and I was back watching the television screen. When Cardinal Bergoglio's name was announced it didn't mean much to me but when I heard the name he was taking, Francisco, I felt my heart fill with joy. The sweet name of my beloved Francis of Assisi!

Would there be any room for a Clare of Assisi? What would this new pontificate mean for the Church and for women like me? We didn't have long to wait to find out. Pope Francis made very clear his position on the ordination of women during a press conference in July 2013: 'The Church has spoken and says no. That door is closed.' It was not unexpected as there was only a slim hope he would have said otherwise.

'The door is closed' is a statement I have heard over and over again, and a reality I have lived with all my life. And yet it was still painful: Here was a new pope, but the same old bad news, the same exclusion. Not for the first time I thought: When did Jesus ever tell his women disciples 'that door is closed?' Who closed it, and who keeps it closed? Men.

Nevertheless, Pope Francis' pontificate was widely heralded as a new springtime in the Church, a quiet revolution. But while he could hear the cry of the poor and respond with compassion, could he not hear the cry of women? Or were the women invisible and their cry, their groan, muffled behind that closed door?

ఎ ఎ ఎ

THE PAINFUL MEMORY OF MY 1994 meeting with Cardinal Daly on the hill in Armagh remained indelibly with me. It had been a most bruising encounter with ecclesiastical power, then at its height. For years I had known I would need to go back to re-visit it, but when and with whom?

The opportunity for healing finally came in early March 2014 in the guise of an invitation to the Celtic Spirituality Centre in Armagh. Its director, a Church of Ireland priest, Grace Clunie, couldn't have been more gracious and hospitable. I shared with her my previous experience, and my desire to pray at the grave of Cardinal Daly.

As we stood in the spring sunshine besides St Patrick's Cathedral, I sensed that after all these years something in me had lifted. 'You laugh a lot,' Grace had commented at the end of our day together. Twenty years earlier I had wept my heart out.

The place of devastation had become a place of resurrection. I drove home filled with gratitude for all the blessings received. But I didn't miss the irony that it was a Church of Ireland woman priest who had accompanied and ministered to me on that day, pace Cathal + Daly!

                ঙ   ঙ   ঙ

I HAVE ONLY ONCE PREACHED AT MASS in a Catholic Church thanks to the Saint Patrick's Missionary Society (Kiltegan fathers) who took a chance on me. I was invited to give a day retreat to priests in May 2014. This meant giving an input in the morning and one in the evening and to be available for one to one spiritual direction sessions if required. I was also asked to preach at midday Mass, and so I prepared accordingly.

When the time for Mass came and I walked into the large chapel filled mainly with priests and a few women, I realised there was a problem. The priest presiding was wearing red, which meant the Mass would be for the feast day of the Apostle Matthias, with the appropriate readings.

I thought I had been told it would be the readings of an ordinary day. So now I wondered anxiously, what text would I have to preach on? As the Gospel was proclaimed, John 15: 9 to 17, I listened very attentively. At least it was one of my favourite Gospel passages.

I took a deep breath before starting. I was aware I was preaching in front of dozens of men, all of whom had delivered thousands of homilies around the world. A priest had told me once that his fellow priests were the severest critics. But there I was: I could only speak the words which were given to me in the moment, deep in my heart.

I spoke of Christ's intimate love for each one of us. The sky didn't fall because a woman had preached at Mass, and I got some good feedback afterwards. One older priest told me, approvingly, that what I said reminded him of something he had read in (Saint) Dom Columba Marmion's books, so obviously I wasn't preaching heresy! The village of Kiltegan is only 20 minutes from Tullow, my first port of call in Ireland, and I thought of the young teenager I was then. But I had felt at home preaching; I was born to do this.

༄ ༄ ༄

On 30 January 2015 the Pontifical Council for Culture, a Vatican body with 31 male members, put on its website the image it had chosen to illustrate its forthcoming plenary assembly on the theme of 'Women's Cultures: Equality and Difference'. When I first saw it, I was shocked by the message it was sending. I decided to print a copy to bring to the evening spirituality lecture I was attending in Milltown. I felt it needed to be shared.

When I showed it to others, mostly women, no one would believe me.

'You are not serious, it's a joke!'

'It can't be . . . you're having us on.'

And indeed, who could blame them for being incredulous?

They were looking at a frontal view of a plaster cast of an amputated nude female torso with the exposed breasts, belly and pubic area tightly bound with rope. There was no head or face, no arms and no legs. A woman in bondage.

'No, I am not joking, this is from the Pontifical Council for Culture.'

The sculpture is called 'Venus Restored' and was made by Man Ray. There were sharp intakes of breath all around.

The smiles disappeared, replaced by anger at what was seen as deeply insulting. What next?

I was encouraged by their reaction to continue bringing this to the attention of others far and wide, and to email the Pontifical Council demanding its removal. The Pontifical Council for Culture got one of its women consultors to defend its choice of image: 'It represents the past as an anchor to generate new ideas.'

As this didn't work in quelling the mounting complaints from around the world, the Council switched from the past to the present. We were informed that:

> While acknowledging the anger, Cardinal Ravasi [the head of the Council] has chosen not to remove the image as it speaks clearly for one of the central points of the document: many women, alas, are still struggling for freedom (bound with rope), their voices and intellect often unheard (headless), their actions unappreciated (limbless).

Obviously, more was needed to communicate our outrage at this representation of male fantasy of domination over women. On 14 February, Valentine's Day, members of We Are Church stood outside the nunciature. We held large placards with the image in full colour and the caption: 'The Vatican's Image of Women. NO!' It certainly captured the attention of motorists passing by.

We even caught the nuncio unaware as he literally ran into us on his way back from jogging around the block. *The Irish Times* report on our protest on 17 February carried an arresting photo of the nuncio in his shorts followed by me with a large placard of 'Venus restored'. On the same day the newspaper also published a piece I had written to raise awareness about the image and the refusal by Cardinal Ravasi to remove it despite widespread criticism.

In Ireland, that image – symbolic of male violence against women – was particularly disturbing as it coincided with the media coverage of a murder trial involving an abusive relationship and the violent death of a vulnerable woman at the hands of a sadistic man.

The Pontifical Council gathered behind closed doors for its Plenary Assembly, 31 male members, mostly clerics, plus a few carefully chosen women. Cardinal Ravasi defended that process as 'women directing the dance, with men performing the steps.' There had been an attempt at broader women's involvement by requesting images depicting our lives, hopes and dreams to be shown at an open day. Mine, and many others, were excluded for representing our call to priesthood. The image of a woman holding a chalice in her hands was obviously far more threatening than a headless, armless torso in bondage. After all, hadn't the Council preparatory document summarily dismissed the issue: 'There is no discussion here of women priests, which according to statistics, is not something that women want.'

On March 10 the Pontifical Council replaced the Man Ray sculpture with a painting by another male artist, 'The Sacred Hour' by Ferdinand Hodler, with four women sitting demurely. 'Venus Restored' had become 'Venus Removed', but women remained the objects of male depictions in pictures and theological statements.

If an image is worth a thousand words, the patriarchal, misogynistic view that denigrates women's bodies and holds women in spiritual bondage had been given full exposure.

☙ ☙ ☙

WHILE MOST CATHOLIC INSTITUTIONS obeyed the Vatican ruling that women's ordination was no longer up for discussion, there were some who showed some courage. I was invited by religion teachers to speak in some Catholic schools across the country, and in one several times. I always found it rewarding to be in the presence of students, to be able to share something of my faith and sense of vocation, and to answer their searching questions. Above all, I tried to encourage them to find their own unique vocations in life and to be true to their deepest selves.

On one occasion in 2017 I was surprised when the teacher said they would show a clip of my 1998 *Late Late Show* appearance, but it was nothing compared to finding out that I had featured in their Religious Education Book on Gender and Religion for the past ten years and didn't know it!

Like St Thomas, I had to see it to believe it. But yes, there I was, complete with a photo of Colm and myself at the 2001 Dublin WOW Conference, in a book published by Veritas. I chuckled when I saw that the copyright belonged to the Irish Episcopal Commission on Catechetics and that it was 'Printed with Ecclesiastical Approval'.

The entry, however, was very fair and comprehensive including my vocational story as well as the threat of excommunication on women celebrating the Eucharist. It certainly was encouraging to know that pupils in Catholic schools across the country had been able to discuss the issue. I certainly had never dreamt I would appear in a religion schoolbook in Ireland!

☙ ☙ ☙

WHEN IT WAS CONFIRMED THAT Pope Francis would be coming to Dublin in August 2018 for the World Meeting of Families (WMF), I had to make a decision: Would I be going to the Papal Mass in the Phoenix Park? I remembered being a steward in 1979 when John Paul II had gathered one million people for the Papal Mass. Thirty-nine years had elapsed and my path had led me to the margins of the institutional Church. I decided that my place would not be at the Mass, but outside. This was especially symbolic as that Sunday was the anniversary day of my baptism.

On a wet Sunday morning, Colm and I and members of Women's Ordination Worldwide stood outside the entrances to the Mass, handing out leaflets for the ordination of women. Later I joined in the Stand For Truth witness rally on Parnell Square and the silent march to the former Magdalen Laundry in Sean McDermott Street in solidarity with survivors of sexual and physical abuse in the Church. I had wondered how I would feel, but deep down it felt right to be there, if not easy.

When it was announced that the World Meeting of Families meeting would be in Dublin, I knew I wouldn't be taking part in the three-day pastoral Congress. But We Are Church had hoped to be able to have a stand there and had applied, with the required deposit paid, but time passed and there was no news of a stand being allocated. Finally, a response came saying there was no room.

A few days later we received a letter confirming what we had guessed. A WMF employee told us he was ashamed we had been lied to, that there was room but we just weren't wanted.

This was later confirmed by Francis DeBernardo of New Ways Ministry who was staying with us while reporting on the World Meeting of Families. There was plenty of room, just not for us or any of the international Catholic LGBTQ+ groups who had also applied.

So We Are Church would be holding events outside, drawing attention to those excluded in the WMF, especially LGBTQ+ members. Indeed, the event I most enjoyed was the Gay choir outside the RDS where the WMF was taking place. There was a wonderful atmosphere and we sang with gusto, as I twirled my rainbow umbrella in New Orleans fashion. I also enjoyed the opportunity for meeting lesbian, gay and transgender Catholics from all over the world.

But what remains most vividly in my mind is the morning of Pope Francis' arrival. I was standing on the Ha'penny Bridge holding a purple umbrella inscribed Women Priests and surrounded by people with other purple umbrellas and an array of rainbow flags in support of the LGBTQ+ community. We had attached bright blue ribbons to the white railings of the bridge in solidarity with survivors of clerical child sexual abuse and they were fluttering briskly. I felt a great sense of purpose, standing on that bridge over the Liffey, like a captain on deck of a ship, looking towards O'Connell Bridge.

A Divine Calling

A young reporter had asked me for a few words. They were syndicated by the Press Association and went around the world. It was a call to open the abuse files.

> Unless the truth comes out, and we know that as Christians, and we know that as Catholics, there is no movement forward, there is no resurrection, there is no transformation and trust cannot be re-established until the truth is acknowledged. It is very painful and it will be very disturbing but the truth is buried in the bottom, in the secret archives, of a lot of dioceses and especially in the Vatican.

ஐ ஐ ஐ

FOLLOWING THE AMAZONIAN SYNOD, in February 2020 Pope Francis issued an apostolic exhortation, Beloved Amazonia (*Querida Amazonia*). After referring to his many ecclesial dreams for the region in inspiring, poetic form, it was a stark contrast when he reaffirmed the exclusion of women from ordination on the basis of an outdated, frozen view of the feminine. I viewed it, as many others did, not as a dream, but as an ongoing nightmare. It was a further confirmation of their distorted patriarchal view of women.

On 8 March, International Women's Day, I was once again outside the nunciature with members of We Are Church to send the message in song, speech and flowers, 'No woman, No Church'. Exactly two years earlier in Rome, Mary McAleese had described the Catholic Church as 'an empire of misogyny'. As I stood holding my St Brigid's Cross listening to Ursula Halligan deliver a powerful speech, I knew I was living the truth of what I had heard in a recent dream: 'I have to live now with women being subordinate in the Church, but I will never accept it.' I then woke up and wrote down those words.

What had struck me most in this vision of the night was the strength of the resolve within me: 'I will never accept it.' I would not settle for Pope Francis' limited dream for women. I was motivated by a bigger dream.

ஐ   ஐ   ஐ

'Why do you want power?' It was the first time I was asked that question, but definitely not the last. I was attending a workshop for priests and lay people in Wicklow Town with Eamonn McCarthy in February 1991. I had mentioned to a priest that I had a calling to the priesthood and his immediate response, spoken with a hint of aggression, was, 'Why do you want power?'

I was taken by surprise. I had never thought of the priesthood in terms of power. It was always referred to as a way of 'serving' in the Church. I thought in terms of sacramental and pastoral work. I still had to hear about the power of governance vested exclusively in the ordained.

I didn't know what to answer, so I replied with a question: 'Is that why you became a priest?' It was the turn of the priest to become silent.

Later I would remember this short exchange as quite emblematic. The same question would be put to me and other women over and over again. I realised that there was a clear double standard at work. When a young man declares his intention to become a priest there is encouragement and praise for his worthy desire to serve. Power isn't mentioned. But when it is a woman, she is immediately accused of being power-seeking. And yet, we are talking about the same ministry.

The other accusation I have often heard is that a woman like me has been contaminated by that dreaded disease of clericalism:

> You only want to be a priest because you don't value your baptism and being a lay person. You think you need to be 'more' or 'better'.

I agree that clericalism is a disease and very damaging, but does that mean that every man who is ordained a priest, a deacon, a bishop thought being baptised wasn't enough? Or, again, does that only apply to women?

Surely, if there is an issue about power and clericalism in the way the ministry is conceived it needs to be addressed. There is no doubt in my mind that baptism is foundational for discipleship and that the Church is a discipleship of equals, in the words of Elizabeth Schüssler Fiorenza. Power needs to be shared across all members of the Church and ministries renewed and redefined.

But to use the issue to justify excluding women from ordination, while continuing to ordain men, is illogical and an abuse of power. Did Pope Francis think he was clericalised (a bad thing) because he answered a call to the ordained ministry? If not, why did he think it would be a bad thing for a woman? Ordain women, or stop ordaining men. Otherwise you are perpetuating an unjust discrimination, a form of gender apartheid.

Whenever I hear the word 'clericalism', I think of an incident from decades ago. I was attending the funeral Mass of a priest. The church where he had been a curate was full.

There was no room in the pews, so I stood at the back on the side of the sanctuary, which was overflowing with priests, several of whom I knew quite well.

When the time came, a ciborium was passed around. None of the priests offered me Communion. I was completely ignored, invisible. With great difficulty I had to make my way through them to join the line of lay people for Communion.

I tried to make sense of it. It was such a contradiction of the Eucharist which is the great Sacrament of love and unity. 'Because there is one loaf, we, who are many, are one body, for we all share the one loaf' (1 Corinthians 10:17). Why could I not receive a host from the same ciborium as the priests? Was it not the same Christ present? Instead of unity, it was a stark affirmation of division, how membership of a clerical caste trumped our common baptism.

            ಠ   ಠ   ಠ

I HAVE ATTENDED THREE ORDINATIONS in my life, none of them mine! The first was a diaconal ordination for a young Columban missionary in the mid-90s in the chapel in Dalgan Park. What remains with me is the surprise of seeing two small women carrying a big carpet roll which they unrolled in front of the altar for the ordinant to lie on. Who was being the servant? Symbolically, the women were the ones.

In October 1996 I went to Paris for the episcopal ordination of Olivier de Berranger, whom I knew from my home parish church. He was on mission in Korea and we had exchanged letters, but our last meeting had been difficult. After morning Mass we had sat in the sunshine outside the church and I had told him about my sense of vocation. He was completely closed to the idea, quite scornful.

'Why can you not be more like the women in Korea? They have kept their femininity.' And then the coup de grace: 'You want everything! You are married, you have children, plus you want to be ordained!'

'It's not me who wants it,' I managed to say in a low voice before dissolving into tears, much to my embarrassment. I felt it was an unfair accusation.

Now he had sent me an invitation to his episcopal ordination in St Denis. I do not know what I expected. When the huge procession of mitres and croziers started into the cathedral I was overwhelmed by the patriarchal, clerical energy. It was as if the oxygen had been sucked out and I could barely breathe. I couldn't wait for it to be over and to get into the fresh air.

And then in 2000 I received an invitation from a young Jesuit friend to attend his ordination in my home town of Versailles. We had got to know Thierry Anne in Dublin and he had taken part in our first prayer vigil for Women's Ordination outside the GPO.

After my previous painful experience in St Denis, I was reluctant to accept, but an elderly Irish Jesuit phoned to ask me if I was going because he couldn't travel on his own. So I said yes.

Over my coat I wore the long purple scarf which is a sign of support for women's ordination, but this didn't prevent me from weeping as the rows and rows of clergy entered. 'It's very male,' Colm commented. It was as painful as I had feared.

The following day was Thierry's first Mass. At least by then I had run out of tears. Afterwards I gave him the relic of St Thérèse I had been given a few weeks beforehand. That was over twenty years ago.

I was invited to another ordination more recently. In 2016, a good friend from college days and Godfather to our younger son was ordained a permanent deacon in Dublin. That time I declined the invitation, regretfully, as I decided not to put myself through that kind of pain again. It was time to spare myself another heartbreak in the midst of general rejoicing. The new deacon and his wife understood and our friendship has endured.

ಬಿ ಬಿ ಬಿ

It was a quiet Sunday evening in March 2021 when the phone rang. 'Did you hear the bishop on the news?' my friend Maureen asked.

'No, why? What did he say?'

'He was interviewed about this new Irish synod. He was asked about women priests, but he said no, there would be parameters. And that's outside the parameters.'

After I put down the phone I listened to the recording. Yes, that's what Bishop Leahy had said, together with the need for managing expectations, of course. After half a century of my expectations being 'managed' by the Church hierarchy, how could I still have any? Maybe it was hope 'outside the parameters' I had, rather than expectations.

Four days previously the Irish Catholic Bishops Conference had announced a Synodal Pathway for the Catholic Church in Ireland. This would lead to a national synodal assembly or series of assemblies within the next five years.

The purpose of this process was to answer the question: What does God want from the Church in Ireland at this time?

Many Catholics, including me, had been asking for some kind of a national assembly for over two decades, and had been promised one, but now the time had finally come.

Undoubtedly the fact that there was increased talk of the Church 'dying', 'being in ruins', 'imploding', 'collapsing' and the number of priests and Church-goers in 'freefall' had contributed to bringing about this Irish Synodal Pathway. There was no denying there was a crisis.

Six months later it was the turn of the Vatican to follow suit with a worldwide consultation when Pope Francis announced in October 2021 a Synod on Synodality. So we were now doubly exhorted to be a listening Church where everyone could speak the truth freely, without fear, boldly, with *parrhesia*, for the sake of the common good. The Spirit was in everyone and had to be heard to discern the path ahead.

All this talk of a listening Church brought back memories of my first experience in 1994 on the Women in the Church subcommittee of the Dublin Priests' Council. As I recounted earlier, this process, designed 'to listen to the pain of women in the Church', ended up compounding this pain for me.

We were now invited to 'trust that this Synodal Pathway was a sincere effort to bring about real transformation and renewal guided by the Spirit', and at the same time we were warned that 'Pope Francis has been clear that synods are not instruments to change Church teachings but rather help to apply Church teachings more pastorally'.

So what hope for somebody like me? I didn't believe that the much needed renewal could happen while insisting that all Church teachings (of various degrees of authority) remained in place. The simultaneous talk of 'reaching out to the peripheries' while making sure that the listening remained within 'the parameters' only served to copper fasten the sense of exclusion I felt.

I had experienced what I called decades of spiritual violence, and there was nothing in this synodal process that was likely to put an end to it. Pope Francis stated repeatedly that the door to women's priestly ordination was shut and would remain shut. And any synod is purely consultative, its decisions having no effect unless ratified by the pope who is the ultimate 'discerner in chief'. So, openness to the Spirit definitely didn't mean openness to women like me who were 'outside the parameters'.

In an article in the *Japan Mission Journal* (Spring 2022) I shared at length these concerns under the title: 'Of Synodality and Closed Doors, Pain and Hope'. The painful reality was that while the synod held the prospect of change and transformation, which I welcomed and supported, it also made it clear that nothing would change in my situation.

In November 2022 Pope Francis gave a lengthy interview in *America* magazine in which he was asked:

> Many women feel pain because they cannot be ordained priests. What would you say to a woman who is already serving in the life of the Church but who still feels called to be a priest?

But Francis skirted around the pain. He chose to answer at a conceptual level, arguing that the Petrine principle showed that ministry was the preserve of men. Women remained excluded from his wide pastoral outreach as if we didn't exist, which of course is the official teaching.

There was no shortage of criticism of the pope's Petrine/Marian principle argument, including in the Vatican's own *L'Osservatore Romano*. Professor Marinella Perroni summarised it best:

> Doesn't the Marian–Petrine principle express an ideology and rhetoric of sexual and gender differentiation that has now been exposed as one of the covers for patriarchal privileges?

Coincidentally, the pope's interview was published on the same day Dr Ann Francis' book, *Called: Women in Ministry in Ireland,* was launched. Her book is based on her extensive research into women's ministry across denominations in Ireland and I am one of the women featured. During the launch discussion one reviewer commented how painful she had found it reading my interview.

Despite the famous official synodal 'parameters', or 'exclusion zones', there was nevertheless a courageous awareness in some quarters that the issue couldn't be completely swept under the Church carpet. The Irish Synodal Synthesis in August 2022 mentioned women's ordination to both the priesthood and the diaconate, as did the Continental Document in October 2022.

The Irish delegation in Prague also included it in its presentation in February 2023. So there was a glimmer of hope that it might be part of the conversation in Rome.

But that faint hope was extinguished when the Working Document (*Instrumentum Laboris*) for the October Synod of

Bishops was published in June 2023, and the issue of women's ordination to the priesthood had been filtered out, or should I say 'discerned out'. Hopes had been raised, however slightly, and then dashed. Two years into the global synodal process, with Pope Francis restating that it was 'a closed question', the synodal office confirmed that 'it was not on the table' for the October 2023 synod meeting in Rome.

I had a marginal involvement in the synodal process, although I kept myself informed, but took an active part in the We Are Church online synodal gatherings and the lay-led Spirit Unbounded synod. Many people expressed gratitude for being asked their views, but I could only say that yes, we have been listened to, but then we are told it's a matter of Church doctrine and can't change.

All this made the following quite a surprise: On 17 August 2022, I was interviewed on RTÉ's 6 O'clock News, commenting on the Synod National Synthesis which had been launched in Knock the day before, especially in relation to women's vocations to priesthood. There had been a phone call from Martin Long of the Irish Bishops Catholic Communications Centre to We Are Church looking for people to answer requests for interviews. I had taken the call and for the first time in my life was doing an interview at the request of the Catholic Communications Centre! I could only conclude this was thanks to the Holy Spirit who didn't deem me 'outside the parameters'!

The Dicastery for the Doctrine of the Faith (formerly the CDF) is the body entrusted with studying 'the question of the necessary participation of women in the life and leadership of the Church'. Unlike the other study groups set up by the synod, we do not know the names of the members, how many there are, how they are selected, and according to what criteria. The Dicastery conducts itself according to procedures established in its own rules, which date back to 1995 and have never been published, all conveniently covered by 'the Pontifical Secret'.

How can one trust the important issue of women's inclusion in ministry in such a secretive and opaque environment? Any call for transparency has been ignored and the DDF is to publish a document later, but only if possible. If it is not possible, one can always set up another confidential commission to defuse this explosive problem called women!

༄ ༄ ༄

WHEN RUTH O'LOONEY OF SCRATCH Films contacted me in early summer 2023 about a documentary they were filming called *The Last Priests in Ireland*, I agreed to participate. Ruth questioned me for about four hours, asking searching questions, and to my surprise I was to be included in the programme. Ardal O'Hanlon was to be the presenter.

One August morning Ruth, Ardal and the Scratch film crew came to the house. As I answered Ardal's questions while being filmed, with the Last Supper behind me, I was totally at ease. In a way it felt like a completely natural thing to do. I just recounted my story. At one stage I became emotional when remembering my anguished prayer while in College: 'Do not call me, your Church doesn't want me.' I had told it many times before, but it was as if I was reliving a pain that has never left since the institutional Church still did not want me.

The Last Priests of Ireland was broadcast on RTÉ on 15 January 2024. I knew my piece would be edited down, but felt that the integrity of my contribution had been preserved. In a film with a male presenter and only men interviewed I stood out as the lone woman. No, I wasn't one of the 'Last Priests in Ireland': I was an emerging new green shoot, even if some would say a weed!

The documentary was followed by a live studio discussion on *Upfront with Katie Hannon*, about the state of the Church in Ireland: Is it dying? I had been asked to sit in the audience. I was tired but managed to address Bishop Brendan Leahy on the panel (the theologian who had argued against women's ordination in RTÉ's *Would You Believe?* in 1995). I spoke clearly of my calling and, conscious of the other women who had not had an opportunity to be heard, ended with, 'we are not cans to be kicked down the road, we are baptised, faithful women, followers of Christ'.

I was not only tired physically, but above all I was tired of decades of exclusion and waiting for change, tired of empty, meaningless words. It must have resonated with some in the audience for I got a round of applause, the only one that evening as it was pointed out to me later on.

When I got home, I again had a sense of 'mission accomplished'. I had shared what I was meant to say. A lot of positive messages awaited me, many commenting that 'it must have taken courage'. But no, it hadn't taken courage, for I had not felt any fear. I was just grateful to have had an opportunity to tell my story. 'What I have whispered in your ear, proclaim from the housetops' (Matthew 10:27).

და და და

THE ISSUE OF SEXUALITY AND CELIBACY was also raised in 'The Last Priests', and while I have experienced a strong calling to the ordained ministry since my teens, I never experienced a call to celibacy as such. When I first felt called I assumed it would include celibacy because that was the way it was generally understood: if one had a calling to the priesthood, one also had a calling for celibacy. The two were inextricably connected.

But I soon realised I didn't have that calling to celibacy. They are different, separate vocations. When the calling to priesthood re-surfaced in 1990, I was already married. I felt that I had been called both to priesthood and to marriage, a conviction which has remained with me all these years.

While I experienced the pain of exclusion, men who had been ordained but had a calling to marriage experienced the pain of having to leave the priesthood. In many cases, they would have loved to continue ministering. Colm and I got to know several of them and their wives in a group called Leaven, for religious and priests who had left the ministry. They welcomed us warmly at their Eucharistic celebrations where these married priests took turns presiding the Eucharist. After a few years they asked me to preside and I was grateful for their recognition of my vocation. Like me, they were trying to follow their calling in an institutional Church which couldn't open itself to change some of its man-made rules.

In January 2024, the Archbishop of Malta, Charles Scicluna, who is the principal investigator of clergy sexual crimes in the Dicastery for the Doctrine of the Faith, called for re-examining the mandatory celibacy rule for priests. He has not done this to remedy the shortage of priests, but because he believes that priests in long-term sexual relationships with women is a global phenomenon which must be acknowledged. He focuses on the plight of individual priests, how this impacts the women and children involved, and the inevitable hypocrisy of pastors living double lives.

One could say that this has been the case for the last millenium, since celibacy became mandatory. It drove the active sexual lives of a lot of clergy underground, with a corresponding loss of integrity. It is generally estimated that around 50 per cent of priests, bishops and cardinals have been involved in sexual relationships of one kind or another. Of course, the other elephant in the room involves clergy engaged in gay sexual relationships.

The mandatory celibacy rule performs the useful function of sweeping all this sex under the carpet, but at the cost of creating a deeply mendacious clerical culture. Only a fraction of priests have a calling to celibacy and actually live it. If all those who don't were to acknowledge it publicly, the present clerical system based on duplicity would collapse immediately.

I know an Irish priest who believes he is being prophetic by being secretly married. He is just one of thousands around the world who have contributed to perpetuating a dishonest situation. Interestingly, Archbishop Scicluna's call has found little echo among other bishops. The long standing fiction seems preferable to facing the truth and bringing in change.

ଓ ଓ ଓ

IN THE 1990s I HAD REPEATEDLY SOUGHT a meeting with Pope John Paul II with no result. After his death I didn't attempt to meet with Pope Benedict XVI. Nor did I try with Pope Francis for the first 10 years of his pontificate. But in 2023, the idea to seek an audience resurfaced in the context of the global synodal process where the key words were 'encounter and dialogue', 'reaching to the peripheries', 'listening to the Spirit', 'speaking with boldness'.

This time I wouldn't just request one for myself, but also for other women who had a sense of vocation to the presbyteral ministry. I enlisted the help of German Benedictine Sister Philippa Rath who had published a book in 2021 in which over one hundred women with a calling to priesthood tell their stories, *Weil Gott Es So Will* (*Because God Wants It*). I selected four other women from Germany, Switzerland and England. They were religious and lay, aged from thirties to sixties. I included a short biography on each one of us.

I wrote to the nuncio in early June 2023 asking him to forward my request to the pope. He replied that every woman had to personally sign the letter. This was done and the request was sent again in July 2023. Separately, I had twice also written directly to the pope at a Vatican address that summer.

The summer passed, with no response to these three letters. Eventually, a letter arrived from the Vatican through the Dublin nunciature dated 4 October (feast of St Francis) from the Substitute, Archbishop Edgar Peña Parra. It was a fairly bland acknowledgement, which made me believe the pope hadn't seen my letter. Not only that, but Archbishop Pena Parra didn't even mention that I had requested an audience.

I decided I would try to get somebody to hand over a letter to the pope personally. But who? Cardinal Hollerich of Luxembourg, a Jesuit, came to mind. Cardinal Hollerich was the General Relator for the Synod and a Member of the C9, the nine cardinals who advise the pope. So I wrote to him explaining my request and asking him to deliver my letter to the pope when he next met him. I included a letter of reference from a former Irish Jesuit Provincial, as well as the article I had written for the *Japan Mission Journal* about my sense of vocation and the global synod.

Cardinal Hollerich met with the pope in early December, at a meeting of the C9, where women in the Church were discussed, and again in January. He would certainly have had the opportunity to hand over my letter to the pope. I wondered whether he had?

As there was no reply from Cardinal Hollerich I finally emailed him in the middle of January 2024 asking him for an acknowledgment and a response. All in vain. At that stage I was ready to give up when a religious sister announced that she was going to Rome soon for an event connected to St Brigid and would be meeting with the pope. I reconsidered: Should I try at least one more time? Would she bring my letter, would she give it to the pope? On the feast of St Brigid she emailed me a photo of herself handing over my letter to Pope Francis who gave her the thumbs up.

It was now April 2024 and the letter handed to Pope Francis on the eve of St Brigid's day, 1 February, had yielded no response. Had he read it at all? Had his private secretary binned it?

Then came the news that Cardinal Grech, the Head of the Global Synod on Synodality, would be coming to Ireland to speak at a two-day conference in mid-April, open to all, in Knock!

Would I make another attempt? Nothing to lose. So Colm went off to Knock to attend the conference with yet another copy, the sixth, of my letter. I couldn't go because these Church gatherings were just too painful. Colm handed the letter over to Cardinal Grech, explaining to him what it was all about. Cardinal Grech listened attentively and promised he would give it to Pope Francis. At the same time Colm gave him a framed copy of 'The Last Supper' by Irish artist Nora Kelly. It had just featured on the front cover of *The Tablet* to illustrate an article by Margaret Hebblethwaite on the presence of women and children at the Last Supper.

Mid-morning on 23 May, an email popped into my inbox, the sender's name arousing my curiosity, Segretaria di Stato Vaticano, and then the subject matter, Respuesta a su carta. I opened the attached pdf file and burst into laughter. It was another bog standard bureaucratic acknowledgment of correspondence, with the obligatory dash of piosity. There was, again, no mention of the content of my letter. It wasn't that the request for a meeting was turned down, it was never even acknowledged.

Why did I laugh? After a whole year and six copies of the letter being sent to the pope in Rome, I should have been disappointed. But, even unknown to myself, I had moved beyond disappointment. Somehow I had reached a stage of no longer expecting anything from the Vatican, not even a reply. I laughed because the emailed acknowledgement was so bland, so *passe-partout*, so conspicuously a 'tick the box' exercise. There wasn't the slightest effort to make it appear personal and important. A whole year of earnest efforts delivered just that: one more automatic assurance of a papal prayer and an apostolic blessing!

I was reminded of my earlier correspondence with John Paul II thirty years previously when Nuncio Gerada had told me, 'your letters do not deserve a reply'. *Plus ça change, plus c'est la même chose.* This was underlined further by the timing: The Vatican response was dated 22 May, the thirtieth anniversary of *Ordinatio Sacerdatolis*.

As if that wasn't bad enough, another papal 'No' made the headlines that very day: 'Pope Francis says No to women being ordained deacons.' That blunt answer was in response to a question from a CBS television interview: 'Could a little Catholic girl dream of someday being ordained a deacon?'

'No!'

As if popes could control little girls' dreams!

'You must be devastated,' a friend asked me, who clearly was.

'No, I am not . . . perhaps it's age,' I ventured. I have been through so much over the past fifty years, since I first received that calling in 1974. 'Maybe I am beyond . . .' Beyond what? I was, puzzled at my own lack of disppointment that so many other women were expressing.

What I know is that I have a strong sense of belonging in the Church, together with an equally strong sense of not having my place in it. As a woman, there is a place assigned to me, a subordinate place, but it's not *my* place, my true place to which God has called me.

ಲ ಲ ಲ

A Divine Calling

IN OCTOBER 2024 THE SYNODAL ASSEMBLY gathered in Rome to issue a Final Document with one whole paragraph (par. 60) on women. I wasn't surprised to hear that this paragraph met the most resistance and received the least support.

> By virtue of Baptism, women and men have equal dignity as members of the People of God.
>
> However women continue to encounter obstacles in obtaining a fuller recognition of their charisms, vocation and place in all the various areas of the Church's life. This is to the detriment of the Church's shared mission . . .
>
> There is no reason or impediment that should prevent women from carrying leadership roles in the Church: what comes from the Holy Spirit cannot be stopped. Additionally the question of women's access to diaconal ministry remains open. The discernment needs to continue . . .

There was of course no mention of the presbyteral and episcopal ministries. I wasn't surprised as it was to be expected: It had been repeatedly asserted that the door remained shut and it wasn't up for discussion.

Pope Francis died on Easter Monday in 2025 and has been succeeded by Cardinal Robert Prevost, now Pope Leo XIV. As the eyes of the world looked upon the streamed funeral Mass for Pope Francis and the inaugural Mass of installation for Pope Leo, women were largely invisible. The conclave, of course, remained as ever a strictly male-only affair.

Pink smoke released by Women's Ordination Conference (WOC) and Women's Ordination Worldwide (WOW) on a hill overlooking the Vatican highlighted the continued marginalisation of the female half of the Church.

I have been asked repeatedly what Pope Leo's election will mean for women like me in the Church? My honest answer is that I don't know, and won't speculate since his pontificate could last 20 years!

I don't read the tea leaves, but of course some commentators do. One headline which has stayed with me from the Associated Press seems to express a general consensus: 'Those who have worked with Pope Leo XIV are optimistic he'll elevate women's roles – with limits.'

With limits!

As the biographical details of Robert Prevost's ministry became known I was particularly struck by the fact that he was a young missionary in Peru at the time of Sister Irene McCormack's martyrdom there. As I recounted earlier, she celebrated the Eucharist, believing that: 'As we gather in memory of Jesus, there is no power or authority on earth that can convince me that Jesus is not present.'

No limits.

May Sister Irene's witness help open Pope Leo's eyes and remove these man-made limits to women's ministry.

We are now preparing for a global Synodal Ecclesial Assembly in Rome for 2028, and before that our own Irish Synodal Pathway Assembly in 2026. As the discernment continues it is my hope that the truth of 'what comes from the Spirit cannot be stopped' becomes a reality. It has been a long time. Now is the time.

This memoir is my contribution, written with *parrhesia* in this Jubilee Year of Hope!

10.

Epilogue

As I was writing this memoir, the death of American Sister Theresa Kane was announced on 22 August 2024. She had made headlines in October 1979 when upon welcoming Pope John Paul II in Washington she challenged him to open all ministries in the Church to women. Later the pope's response to the issue of women's ordination was to dismiss it jokingly with, 'It's a long, long way to Tipperary'.

Yes, it's a long, long way and generations of women in Ireland and around the world have been treading it. It's a long, long way, but Tipperary does exist, and there is a way to get there.

On hearing my story many people ask, somewhat in disbelief: How do you keep going after all these years? I have often wondered myself. It's a cliché to answer 'one day at a time', but it is nevertheless true: one day at a time, putting one foot in front of the other. It's just as well I didn't know years ago how long the way would be. It's a marathon, with hurdles, and uphill all the way!

I have often thought of the title Nelson Mandela gave to his autobiography, *Long Road to Freedom*, for indeed this too is like a long road to freedom, a road many women have travelled before me, and a road I walk with others and for others.

Epilogue

I have a strong sense of mission. Like Jeremiah, I have tried at times to refrain from speaking out, but 'there was a fire in my bones' I couldn't quench. I also have been blessed to know countless people of all ages and genders who have inspired me and given me support in so many ways. Of necessity, only very few are mentioned by name in this memoir, but each has contributed to helping me walk this long path to freedom. And then there have been special companions on the journey: my husband, soul friends, and members of what we call the Communion of Saints on earth and in heaven.

From childhood nature has always been a source of refreshment and healing for me, and it is a gift to be living between the mountains and the sea. Both have witnessed my tears, absorbed my anger, soothed my spirit, aroused my wonder, stretched my body. From the time I first discovered Glendalough as a child it has been a special place for me. And my love for Connemara with its wide skies, wild coast and cloud reflections in the lakes has never left me: my spirit is at home in wild places.

Books, of all kinds, have enriched my life enormously. From the time I read at night under my bedcover as a child they have given me sustenance. I am particularly in debt to the mystics of all ages and faiths (and none) whose writings have made my heart sing. One quality not listed as a gift of the Spirit, but should be, is a sense of humour! As a teenage student I had on my wall a poster of a clown with the caption: 'Don't take yourself too seriously!' Very wise advice.

While I seem to have an endless capacity to shed tears, I also find plenty to laugh at in life: My God is a playful God and a God of mirth. Art, poetry, dance and the joy of music lift me, and I delight in the song and flight of birds. Above all, I take great pleasure and joy in the One who loves me and all of creation.

> Yes, brother John Paul,
> And brother Benedict,
> and brother Francis too,
> and now brother Leo,
> it's a long, long way to Tipperary,
> but we are getting there,
> and women, and all, will be free!

Magnificat!

27 June 2025
Feast of the Sacred Heart

Select Bibliography

- The Wijngaards Institute website, womenpriests.org, is the world's most comprehensive Internet resource on the subject.

- *Women's Ordination in the Catholic Church* (Cascade Books, 2020) by John O' Brien shows how the ordination of women represents a necessary pastoral-theological development.

- *What About Me? Women in the Catholic Church* (Mercier Press, 2018) is an insightful personal exploration of the place of women in the Church .

- *Called* (Wipf & Stock, 2022) by Anne Francis is the fruit of her research on women engaged in Christian ministry in Ireland across denominations.

- *The Curia Is The Pope And Why it Cannot Listen* (Mount Salus Press, 2020) by John O'Loughlin Kennedy has a well documented chapter on the priestly ordination of women.

- *The Elephant in the Church* (Columba Press, 2014, revised 2019) by Mary T. Malone explores what she calls 'Women Christianity' from a historical perspective.

And for the Francophiles:

- *Le Déni* (Bayard, 2014) by Maud Amandier and Alice Chablis shows how in the Church men have power and women serve.

Acknowledgements

The seed for *A Divine Calling* was planted over 20 years ago when my friend the late Sacred Heart Sister Madeleine Sophie McKee told me, and not just once: 'You should write your story, like St Thérèse did'.

'Well, I am not St Thérèse!' I replied, but of course the idea was slowly taking root. Later, another friend, Josie O'Reilly, made sure to water that seed with repeated encouragement that there was indeed a story to be written. Thank you Josie for your persistence overcoming my procrastination, and for ploughing through that still rather rough early draft. Your affirmation and feedback kept me going through the necessary long revising process, but also told me when to stop!

Much of my contemplative pondering behind *A Divine Calling* took place during the Quiet Garden retreat days facilitated by Cynthia Bailey Moran. Thank you Cinnie for that beautiful, peaceful supportive space where the silence is pregnant with Spirit. Thank you for reading the draft and sharing your deep spiritual wisdom born of experience. You have given me so much.

Many thanks to Mary McAleese for her long-standing support and for contributing a Foreword which reflects

Acknowledgements

her own fierce commitment to women's equality in the Catholic Church.

I am also very grateful to David Givens of The Liffey Press for his interest and diligence in publishing my story. He has ventured where angels, or rather religious publishers, feared to tread. I believe that it is no coincidence our first meeting took place on 25 March, world day of prayer for women's ordination.

I couldn't have written this memoir without the spiritual support of the one who has been my Anam Cara for over fifty years, Eamonn McCarthy. There is no greater gift than to be believed and Eamonn was the first to do so. Thank you for your steadfast friendship which did cost you, your ever patient listening ear, and the assurance of your prayers. There was little in that draft you read you didn't know already.

Forty-five years ago when I married Colm Holmes, little did he know that he was embarking on a strange adventure. Thank you Colm for your loving, supportive presence at my side; *A Divine Calling* is in many ways also your story. I am grateful that you kept detailed diaries, such useful aide-mémoire for some events no longer so fresh in my memory. And of course your computer skills turned my messy drafts into a presentable manuscript. We are a team.

Many more people have helped me to bring this book to fruition than I can name here. But your kindness is not forgotten and I am grateful to each one. I hope the book does not disappoint your rather high expectations: It is not St Thérèse's Story of a Soul, pace Sr Madeleine Sophie!

And finally, to Tadhg and Fionn, our little grandsons who really didn't help at all at all with this book: Thank you for just being you and a very lively reminder that the Kin-dom of God belongs to children. I pray you find your own unique divine calling in life. There is no greater happiness.

Dieu merci. Buíochas le Dia.